Reflections on a River

(*Photo: E. T. Atkinson*)

A peaceful stretch of the Lambourn

HOWARD MARSHALL

Reflections on a River

Illustrated with drawings by the author and Ernest Petts

H. F. & G. WITHERBY LTD
61 WATLING STREET · LONDON EC4

First published 1967

SBN 85493 000 0

Printed in Great Britain by
Ebenezer Baylis and Son Limited
The Trinity Press, Worcester, and London

For Jasmine –
Whose powers of persuasion and genuine interest made it impossible for me to avoid writing this book.

H.M.

Contents

List of Illustrations

I

The Little River

ALWAYS I come back to the little River Lambourn. The fact that I am fortunate enough to live on its banks is beside the point. If I lived a hundred miles away I should still return to this limpid stream and its golden trout. These trout are not big, but they are plump and wild and beautifully shaped, and they weed you more swiftly and decisively than any trout I know. The river is a chalk stream in miniature, with all the characteristics of its bigger brothers the Kennet, the Test and the Itchen. Indeed, it flows into the Kennet through a dark and inconspicuous culvert beneath the Bath Road, and a friend of mine who lived on this modest confluence caught with a dry fly, and standing virtually on his own doorstep, a noble trout, deep and thick and weighing six-and-a-quarter pounds.

Such visiting leviathans provide the charm of the unexpected, but we do not altogether welcome them. They are out of scale. They destroy the proportion of things. Last September I put a fly over a quiet dimple under the far bank, and a great neb came up and absorbed it and turned down. When I tightened, after a delay caused more by shock than good timing, I felt momentarily that I had hooked a brick wall. Then there was a vast boil and an explosion and a huge trout leapt clear of the water, skeetered along on his shovel of a tail and came down fairly and squarely and conclusively on my 5x nylon.

He was a big fish. A very big fish, certainly over four pounds, and yet, as I watched the waves spreading where he indignantly shouldered his way upstream like an All Black forward driving through a maul, I was not altogether sorry. A little sad at my own usual incompetence, perhaps, but this visitor from the Kennet, searching for spawning grounds, was right out of his league. He had nothing in common with my lively little trout. He made my river look like a ditch. I was glad to see the last of him.

Sour grapes, you may say, but I really do not think so. Had I lost as large a fish on the Kennet, I should have been more than sad. There such a fish would have fitted into the pattern. He would have been expected, and the angler would have been equipped to deal with him. Not that equipment is enough.

The margin of human error is wide, and we are all potential bunglers with a fly rod in our hands.

Especially when we find a great trout rising steadily, and our knees begin to tremble slightly and our breathing is somewhat irregular and our fingers refuse to deal with the minor intricacies of a half blood knot. Especially then are we liable to bang the fly down so heavily over the trout's head that he sidles contemptuously under the nearest weed bed to take cover until we have gone. Trout are downright insulting when they do this. They show no panic. They merely let us see that they are perfectly aware of our intentions, but that there is a limit to their patience. This can be rather humiliating if it happens too often. It can even lead to bad temper.

I remember an otherwise tranquil friend of mine who suffered this indignity rather frequently under a July sun, until suddenly he cried, 'I did not come here to be sneered at by a trout. I shall never fish again', and with that he tried to make the ritual gesture of breaking his rod and hurling it into the river. Unfortunately he was using a tough, glass rod, and strain though he might he could make no impression on it, no satisfactorily dramatic smash, no sharp splintering sounds. All he could do, in this faintly ricidulous situation, was to yield to his sense of humour and continue to fish.

For all that, I know how my friend felt. In this little river the water is so pellucid and so relatively shallow, that the angler can see every happening, every pebble in the golden gravel, every movement of a fin. Looking at a trout poised motionless in a run between weed beds you might think you were looking at a Chinese water painting, and when you cast your fly, however delicately, the falling nylon seems to splinter the crystal surface into a cracked windowpane. All this, of course, is part of the delight of this miniature fishing, and gives it, as Yeats said, 'the fascination of what's difficult'.

It poses also certain problems of equipment. The weaver's beam which served our forefathers as a rod in all conditions, would be sadly out of place. It was evolved, this stiff, heavy, powerful type of rod, to cope with the downstream winds which blow so often on the chalk streams, and doubtless served its purpose. But at what a cost of fishermen's elbows and weary wrists I would not like to say. The great G. E. M. Skues was a protagonist of the less ponderous rod, though even he thought he was fishing fantastically light when he used the W.B.R. – the world's best rod, as he called it – a nine foot Leonard weighing about six ounces. He preached the doctrine that lightness of delivery is all, and he noted with approval that a two-and-a-half pound trout was taken in heavily weeded Itchen water on a little Leonard weighing only two-and-a-half ounces.

It is a fact of no earth-shattering importance, but I find myself using a split cane rod six feet ten inches long and weighing only a quarter of an ounce more than that little Leonard. I came to this by stages. First an old rugger injury caught up with me and put my right arm out of action, so that I had to learn to cast with my left. This was for me most interesting, since all the casting tricks which I had practised intuitively with my right hand had to be analysed, rationalized and deliberately applied with the left hand. I was never a good caster, and now I never shall be one, but I catch a trout now and again and at least I know what I am trying to do. And one of my endeavours is to make up for loss of distance by fishing as lightly and delicately as possible. Not that I succeed very often, but a tiny, tooth-pick of a rod at least makes it feasible.

It must be a sympathetic tooth-pick which will persuade the fly out even into a wind. A little, stiff poker of a rod is useless. Fly fishing should be a matter of finesse rather than force, and when you find yourself stroking the line out with a rod which works down to the hand, things are not going so badly.

There is, I believe, a tendency towards the use of shorter and lighter trout rods, a tendency which justifies itself at the end of a day's hard casting into a headwind. It presupposes a different approach to fly fishing, a search for the trout within range instead of an exercise in tossing the caber.

The great casters will smile (tolerantly, I hope) at this whimsy. Men like Cecil Terry and Harry Tetlow will continue to send their lines whistling across the widest reaches of the Kennet to take the unapproachable trout under the far bank. They are wonderful to watch, these Cinquevallis of the fly rod, and they catch big fish. But I know my place. I could not at any time emulate them and it is a considerable relief not to have to try.

On the little river there is no room for emulation, and nothing calls for tests of physical prowess. Our problems are within range given a little low cunning and a modicum of skill. It is true that we may have to creep and crawl a bit to keep under cover, and that the banks are marshy in places and may claim a gumboot or two before they let us go. And there are cattle. And nothing could be more exasperating than a herd of bullocks. Inquisitive bullocks. And they are always inquisitive. These hazards, however, are common to any trout stream, and with them are invariably to be found such irritants as horse flies, herons, swans, ducks, moorhens, dabchicks and the rest. Sometimes, when you are doing badly, and a north-east wind is tearing and buffeting its way downstream, sometimes you feel that you must be fishing in a kind of lunatic zoo, with all the inmates dancing derisively around you.

The fact is that you rarely notice these manifestations of nature. It is often said that one of the virtues of trout fishing is that it gives you glimpses of wild animals and birds in their natural environment. The drumming of the snipe over the water meadows, or the eerie cry of the plover in spring, are supposed to compensate us for standing up to our knees in mud with our fly firmly fixed to the branch of a tree behind us just as we have found a rising fish. It may be so. The man of creative imagination may find his consolation in the flash of a kingfisher, but for most of us the fishing is the thing. I do not suppose that the stockbroker, escaping from the city at the weekend, drives eighty miles and dresses up in thigh boots and a fishing jacket, and a most peculiar waterproof hat in order to hear the drumming of the snipe. He knows that fishing consists of a series of misadventures interspersed by occasional moments of glory, and that, to achieve the glory, he must concentrate on the matter in hand.

Concentration is the secret of success, and it is remarkable how anglers cultivate this rare habit of mind. I remember once in Africa, using the aerial from a scout car for a rod and trying to catch anything in the yellow river that swirled at my feet. I was startled by the voice of a game warden. 'I hope,' he said, 'that the elephants did not disturb you?' 'Elephants?' I said. 'What elephants?' 'Oh,' replied the warden, 'a herd of about thirty passed about twenty yards behind you just now on the way to a drinking pool. We were quite worried about you for a bit.' I did not wonder that they were worried about me. I should have been worried about myself if I had known, but I was concentrating and I caught some of the most villainous-looking fish I had ever seen.

There are, I think, two main classes of fly fishers, the Rushers and the Stickers. The Rushers are haunted by the belief that there is always a better fish rising round the next corner, so they are ever on the move, rushing up the bank from rise to rise, confident that one day they will come upon Moby Dick. The Stickers are either more patient or more lethargic men, and having found what seems to them a promising place they stay there and wait for the trout to show themselves.

If I am a Sticker, and I think I am, it is partly through laziness, and partly because there is no place for Rushers on the little river. They would go through it like a knife through butter, and put down all the fish for the rest of the day. You cannot take liberties with the little river, or its trout. If you do not move slowly and stealthily, like an overweight Red Indian, the fish will scatter before you, sending their brethren to cover as they go. It is indeed wiser not to move at all for considerable periods, but to wait and watch for the movement under water or the dark shapes sliding out from beneath the weed beds to take up position before the main hatch of fly begins.

And it is surprising how many trout will appear in a stretch which an hour before seemed to hold no fish whatever. But then trout are surprising creatures. The other day I was watching a small boy throwing bread to ducks from a road bridge when suddenly a large trout loomed up from the depths of the bridge pool. He took a quick look round to size up the situation and then launched himself into the attack. He snatched pieces of bread from under the ducks' bills. He rammed ducks amidships like a torpedo. He spread such alarm and confusion among the ducks that they withdrew angrily and left him to feast alone, but having asserted his sovereignty he sank, slowly and with dignity, into the dark recesses of his domain.

But for the boy and the bread I should never probably have seen that trout, except perhaps in may-fly time, but I do not like the may-fly fortnight on my tiny chalk stream. It is useful, maybe, for reconnaissance purposes, for marking down big fish in the hope that they will be moving to blue-winged olive or sedge later in the year; but for fishing it is a mockery. In so small and clear a stream it is too easy. It is murder. It robs the trout of all caution and nullifies the hazards which make fishing in this water so fascinating. This great fly, drifting like a galleon under full sail, this remarkable fly gets everything out of perspective and I could well do without it altogether. Indeed I do manage to do without it – by going to fish elsewhere during the fortnight, by wrenching myself away to places where the contrast is sharpest, to the great trout of Sheelin or the enchanted lochs of Perthshire. But always I return, and always the deep feelings of relief and gratitude accompany me to the marshy banks of the little river.

II

The Eccentric Trout

WHERE the clear water runs deep and steady by a bed of reeds, there lived a trout of substantial size. By now he would be well over four pounds. His name was Sammy, and every visitor who came to fish the Lambourn with me was shown exactly where he was. Sometimes Sammy obliged with a porpoise roll that moved so much water that it set my guests trembling with excitement. Sometimes he made a small dimple on the surface as an olive disappeared, and onlookers made serious miscalculations about his weight.

Sammy was big, there is no doubt of that, and he

had taken up an almost impregnable position. To reach him from a tree-lined bank a roll cast was necessary, and when that had been accomplished there was a most tricky drag problem to surmount. Sammy had seen so many flies whisked away from his nose just as he was about to take them that he made a very leisurely choice now, a most careful and detailed inspection. You could almost see him sneering as a Greenwell or a Gold-ribbed Hare's Ear floated towards him. 'Wait for it – wait for it!' he would say, drifting down below the fly, and when it was suddenly dragged sideways Sammy was not above giving it a parting wallop with his shovel-sized tail.

Most rivers have their Sammy or two, tantalizing monsters who mock us as we deploy all our skills against them. I will admit to having been broken twice by Sammy, once on the strike, the second time after a heavy plunge into a weed bed. It is true that I was using 5x, but among my many fishing faults that of being broken by a fish is the most unlikely to occur. It is just that Sammy, like others of his kind, has established himself in a position which causes us to stretch ourselves to the utmost, and so reduces to microscopical dimensions the margin of error.

He is really just beyond comfortable casting range, and wise men would say that, this being so, we should leave him alone or at least use a thicker leader. They may be right, but anglers are notorious for refusing to take advice. A fish like Sammy is an irresistible challenge, and one day a man endowed with great skill or over-riding luck will drag him from his holt. I shall try hard to be generous when my guest brings Sammy home in triumph, but my smile will be a little wintry, and it will be a struggle to say, in tones of warm generosity, 'Why, that must be Sammy you've got there. Well done indeed!'

The truth is that those of us who live by a river come to know their trout very well, and form for the more lordly ones among them a real affection. I remember, when I first came to the Lambourn, Frank Sawyer saying to me, 'The longer you live here, the less you'll fish and the more you will watch.' And he was absolutely right, as he so often is. There is, after all, so much to watch, not perhaps with the rare and dedicated clinical absorption of David Jacques, whose admirable book, *Fisherman's Fly*, I commend most earnestly to all chalk stream fishermen, but with the general enjoyment of a man who has dined well and is savouring a congenial evening at the play. Fishing is so much more than merely catching fish. It is, by the clear waters of the Lambourn, an involvement in the life cycle of insect and fish, a participation in the organic growth of everything in the valley. From the caddis to the sedge, from the darting nymph to the emerging may-fly, everything is part of a living pattern in which the angler participates.

I stress the clarity of the Lambourn water, for this is important. It enables the angler to watch trout as if they were goldfish in a bowl, though it is one thing to move quietly and observe as you go, but quite another to raise an arm or show a rod in the action of casting. You will then have no trout to fish for or to observe for a very long time. With caution, however, it is possible to creep up to within arm's length of a fish, and very profitable and interesting some of these Red Indian exercises can be.

I remember lying on my face by the Lambourn peering down through the rushes at a fine trout weighing about two pounds, who was behaving, it seemed to me, with a certain amount of eccentricity. He was lying near the surface and close behind a bed of weeds, and every few minutes he would gather himself together and leap a foot in the air clear of the water which he re-entered with a resounding splash. Seen from a distance it might have seemed as if he were trying to cleanse himself of some parasite, but he was being much more constructive than that. He was leaping up and forward, landing every time in the patch of weed, and then hurrying round to grab the nymphs which he had shaken free. I felt that a fish with such reasoning powers should be left to his own devices, and I crept away and left him to his acrobatic meal, hoping that a trout of his mental calibre would become, in due course, another Sammy. My point is, though, that I should not have been able to see this apparently calculated and intelligent performance if the water had not been so pellucid.

Sometimes, when the air is still and the light is kindly, the trout seem to hang poised in a great block of the palest green jade. You can almost see their thought processes, the eager swaying to and fro when nymphs are on the move in their food channel, the stiffening up into a barely perceptible trembling as they become aware of some threatened danger, the final shake and shrug and heave of the shoulders when they sidle away to the shelter of a weed bed. The grayling is almost more informative, erecting his great dorsal fin as he darts forward to intercept a nymph or burrows into the silt, the swivelling turn with which he follows a fly on the surface, and the final upward lunge as he decides to take it.

There are many grayling in the Lambourn. Some would say too many, but I have a great affection for them. They breed too quickly, it is true, and have to be kept down, but they provide most interesting fishing during the winter months. These Lambourn grayling are peculiarly difficult to catch, as Frank Sawyer would confirm. I have watched that great man, who normally on the Hampshire Avon takes a sack when he goes grayling fishing, and only ceases to fish when it is full, I have seen him attacking a shoal of my grayling when they were really moving, and ending up after an hour or so with one small fish and a sense of deeply puzzled frustration.

If I may use an ugly but descriptive word, these grayling in this clear and relatively shallow river are most easily alerted. The shallowness may have something to do with it, for the shadow of line and cast is thrown more clearly upon the river bottom, and this must be a warning. In other deeper rivers, when grayling are disturbed or frightened, they mill madly around and take some time to settle again, but not so on the Lambourn. Here they do not panic. They may jerk sideways when a nymph is dropped too close to them for comfort, but in the main they continue feeding and treat the angler with infuriating disdain.

What is more, they are extremely quick to detect the artificial food offering.

This season I actually caught a couple of grayling early on, using a medium olive on the surface. Since then, on appropriate occasions during hatches of olives I have floated the same fly over that same shoal many times, but never a rise has resulted. They had learnt about the medium olive. It had signalled danger to them and so it is with all the other flies and lures that I have put before them. The odd fish may take a fly he has never seen before but thereafter that same fly is useless. There was a time when I had some moderate success with an 00 pheasant-tail nymph, but not now.

The fact is that these grayling are alerted, and therefore allergic to anything which does not conform most closely to the natural insect with which they are familiar. And not only must it conform in appearance, but its movements and actions must be those of a real nymph or dun. Frank Sawyer is an adept at imparting movement and life to a nymph just before it reaches a fish, but even this is not enough. I have watched grayling after grayling following his nymph downstream with the greatest curiosity, but somehow in the end they always sheered away and returned to their stations.

I have only seen one man who has been relatively successful with these grayling, and that is Dr Cecil Terry, using a coch-y-bondhu type fly of his own devising, but then he takes great pains to conceal himself from the fish, and that, I suggest, is where the rest of us, plagued perhaps by stiffness and infirmity, find it difficult to emulate him. I do not worry about the choosiness of my grayling, for they present a most pleasantly tantalizing problem through the dark months of the year. There is nothing better, to my mind, than an autumn day's grayling fishing, though I must admit that it would be satisfactory, now and then, to come home with a trophy or two.

There are, of course, more practical ways of keeping the grayling down. There is, for example, electro-fishing; and I have heard tales of a thousand fish being removed in a day down at Bagnor. I am, however, not altogether happy about the final effects of electro-fishing and, anyway, the destruction on my water would be far too drastic. Netting, I think, is preferable and quite efficient, and so is wiring the grayling out by slipping a noose over them and drawing it tight with an upward sweep of the arms.

One other method which I have tried successfully is to step into the river in thigh waders some way above a shoal and stir up the silt on the bottom so that it muddies the water. Then, using the finest nylon and a single maggot, you may take grayling after grayling within five feet of your waders. This may not be drastic enough for those who would have all the grayling out, regarding them as pestilential interlopers in a trout stream, but it suits me and helps to keep a reasonably balanced population in the river.

III

Avoiding the Weeds

THIS digression about the teasing grayling enables us to make certain deductions about the character of the river. It is the type of river which suits grayling uncommonly well, and it is also a late river, so that trout are not really in condition until May or thereabouts. By the same token, rainbow trout thrive in it and it is one of the very few English rivers where they are known to breed. It is a river where the behaviour of both trout and grayling suggests that concealment for the angler is of primary importance.

When I first took over my stretch, the banks had been long untended, and very often you had to fish from a screen of reeds, four or five feet high, thus having concealment forced upon you. My diary shows that I caught far more trout in those early days when cover was so much more abundant than I have done since the river keepers have been at work trimming down reeds and cleaning up the banks, and, at the same time, making the angler more visible to fish. It is a strange thing, but few of my guests seem to regard concealment as particularly important. They stand up in full view of the fish in the most confident manner and are surprised when their quarry does not respond. This may be because the river itself has a trusting, peaceful look about it, so that the fish, lying so visibly upon the gravel, are expected to be co-operative and complacent. It may, of course, be due to my own bad example, or perhaps, I should say, my own laziness, and also to the need for avoiding positions which cause my bones to protest painfully.

Now and again I am sharply reminded that age is not on my side. The other day I managed to deceive a vigorous pound-and-a-half rainbow trout who was busily rising at invisible insects under the far bank. For once in a way I struck properly and hooked him firmly, and in the best rainbow manner, he cavorted all over the river. It was only when he began to tire, and I reached for my landing net, that I realized the bank on which I was standing was some four feet above the level of the river, and that, therefore, I had little chance of reaching him with my net. There were trees on each side of me and I could not possibly lead him to a more convenient place. This meant that

I had, by agonizing degrees, to lower myself first to my knees and then full length on to my stomach, at the same time playing a fish which continued to make the desperate last-minute rushes for which rainbows are notorious. It was the best part of twenty minutes before that fish was safely in the net, and it felt like very nearly another twenty before I managed to hoist myself up on my feet again. Mind you, though this kind of performance is painful and nerve-racking, it adds zest to the capture of a trout, and it emphasizes the principle that it is best to plan where you will land your fish before you begin casting to him.

The sad fact is that my days for creeping and crawling are over, and I have to try to catch visible trout on the hop with the first cast before they are alarmed. This is all very elementary, but I am often surprised how really good trout fishermen are apt to be careless and to neglect some of the elementary principles. I neglect them myself in a shameful way. How often, I ask myself, do I test my nylon and tie the fly on anew after playing a relatively heavy fish in weedy water? The answer is, not nearly as often as I should, and more than one good trout owes his freedom to this carelessness.

Incidentally, the Lambourn trout make very cunning use of weed. I remember, when a famous fly fisherman first fished the river with me, and fished it most beautifully, casting unerringly with always enough slack to avoid drag, he quite quickly rose and hooked four good trout, each one of which left his fly deep in a bed of ranunculus. 'Never,' he said, 'have I been weeded so quickly by any trout anywhere.'

And there is no doubt that fish in a shallow, clear river are more accustomed to taking swift, evasive action than those where there is depth of water in a heavy stream. The secret on the Lambourn is not to play a big fish too hard, but to treat him very lightly and steer him gently between the weed beds. You can avoid much peril by following this technique.

One of my guests had lost fish after fish and was becoming despondent until I advised him to try guiding them to his net. I left him to his own devices and by the end of the morning he had taken four good trout averaging a pound and a half. He had, as he told me afterwards, played each fish for about half-an-hour before leading it gently into his landing net. That perhaps was an exaggerated application of the gentle method, but it clearly worked and gave my friend a well-earned feeling of triumph. On other rivers I like to hustle a trout into the net as soon as possible, but on the Lambourn I have found that gentleness pays.

It is easy to be dogmatic about angling techniques, but it is also apt to be unwise. There are so many variables in fishing that what might be right on one stretch of a river, may be disastrously wrong on the next. So many are the varying factors involved that the taking of each fish is a separate and unique event. Every day on the river provides you with more material for clinical observation, and observation properly and progressively applied is the secret of all development in angling.

I would not, however, have angling overlaid with science. It would be heresy to say so on the chalk streams, I know, but many a man fishes with one pattern of fly in different sizes throughout the season. Richard Threlfall, for example, who wrote a delightful book on game fishing called *On a Gentle Art*, uses mainly one pattern of his own devising, in appropriate sizes, all the year round. This is a bushy, hackled, palmered pattern, reddish or black in colour, and with it he catches as many trout, in all conditions, as the next man, and decidedly more than most of us. I am not citing him as an argument against the chalk-stream school of exact imitation. Those who adhere to this school are led by their entomological leanings into fascinating byways. And not necessarily byways. Highways sometimes, as when Skues developed and propounded the art of chalk-stream nymph fishing. And entomological research is not confined to the chalk streams. Wherever there are rivers or lochs or reservoirs there are men who study fly-life and apply the results of their observations by tying, as nearly as they can, copies of the natural insect. This is an inevitable and essential part of the development of fly-fishing, wet or dry. And those of us who have not the great patience or ability required for the researches of a Halford or a Skues are fortunate in that we can follow or experiment with their findings. We do indeed owe them a great debt of gratitude.

I have never understood the tendency to sneer at the chalk-stream purist who restricts his method of trout fishing to the use of the dry fly. David Jacques put his attitude very clearly when he wrote in *Fisherman's Fly*: 'As for myself, I am not particularly interested in killing trout. What does interest me immensely is catching trout by a method called dry-fly, a method that is so intriguing, so full of perplexities and uncertainties, that the actual capture of the fish fades into insignificance compared to the mental stimulation involved. Therefore, I fish where this method is practised exclusively, where I can converse with others who think like I do on problems of mutual interest.'

That, I think, is admirably said. It is a matter of individual choice. There is nothing snobbish about the dry-fly purist. He is simply a man who finds his greatest pleasure in one particular branch of fly-fishing, and that is all there is to it. The great Halford was typical of the purists when he refused to fish any longer with the Gold-ribbed Hare's Ear because he did not know exactly what it represented. The rest of us console ourselves with the thought that it may appear to the fish like an emerging dun, but that anyway the trout find it eatable.

There are times, of course, when we have to cease to use some fly or lure for other good reasons. I remember once being given a large, hairy Sedge tied by that fine all-round fisherman, Terry Thomas. It was a formidable-looking creature, and I tried it in very difficult conditions, with the sun blazing down from a brassy July sky. It proved so deadly, fished awash in the surface film, that I knew that, if I could cover a fish adequately with it, it would almost certainly be taken. It brought up the most stubborn trout with a wallop, and I had to give up using it because it seemed almost unfair and the trout, after all, were my own stock and there had to be a limit.

I thought then that Terry Thomas had put me on to the panacea for all difficult conditions and that, when the trout were dour, I had only to produce this powerful fly to draw them inevitably from the water. Just to show how contrary fish can be, or how mystifying is the art of angling, I decided to try this same fly exactly one week later at the same time of day in precisely similar conditions; windless, blazing sun, great heat and low water – and instead of taking the fly with monotonous regularity, I found that trout turned away from it in rippling panic as it floated down to them.

Now what had happened? Why was the fly, which had been infallible the week before, now, instead of being the extractor, being the intimidator of trout? Clearly, although the conditions were superficially the same, there was some difference of light or underwater life which I had not observed, some fault in my casting or some change in the flow of the river or its height causing invisible drag. I never did find the answer to this problem. I have some theories, of course, but they are too bizarre to be enunciated. They belong among the wilder reaches of the imagination, where they join many others which can be taken down and dusted and inspected with a smile on the days when the river is difficult.

The chalk-stream purist, for whom I have so great a regard, will not have approved of the story of the Sedge, nor will he be able to repress a shudder at the thought of an American artificial fly entitled the Panama appearing on his river. Charles Ritz speaks highly of the Panama and it is a very popular lure in the United States, though no one can say what it is supposed to represent. It is tied with a green body ribbed with yellow, with red hackles and whisks, and it sits up well on the water and is very easily visible. When I had it out during a hatch of olives, the trout took it greedily. It might almost be said that they preferred it to the natural, a fact which would break the purist's heart, or at least take a sizeable chip out of it. There is no explaining the attraction of this fly, though it must lie somewhere with its shape, and with the animation given to it by the length and disposition of its hackles.

I have, more and more, come to the conclusion that, in the presentation of a dry fly to a fish, animation can be at least as important as size and colour. We all know that by skittering a sedge along the surface, we can tempt the trout to make a snatch at it, or that by lifting a nymph in the water, we can attract the grayling. While it is generally important, though, that a trout fly should swim naturally and without drag, it is, in my view, no less important in certain circumstances, that either the angler or the quality and tying of its hackles should give it some degree of apparent life as it approaches a trout. This, I think, is an aspect of dry-fly fishing which has not yet been sufficiently explored or, at least, discussed. Major Oliver Kite and Richard Walker have written interestingly about the problem, and I have no doubt that individual anglers experiment with animating their flies but anglers are, on the whole, individualists and do not lightly pass on the results of their experiments to others.

If we watch a natural fly floating down the stream, we see that it has moments of considerable activity, fluttering its wings, skating here and there, attempting all the time to take off. It follows, moreover, every minute change of direction caused by the current, and only for relatively short distances does it stay still, drying itself preparatory for flight. I have no doubt that, if animation can be given to an artificial fly in the right conditions, it may induce a fish to take, but the movement has to be very slight and natural and well timed.

IV

The Persistent Fisherman

THE river rises in the chalk downs above the village of Lambourn, and near its source there is a pumping plant which extracts water from the springs. This abstraction of water is largely responsible, I do not doubt, for the fact that the Lambourn runs practically dry as far down as Great Shefford after a year in which the rainfall has been low. It is said that trout of up to seven pounds in weight have been found stranded in the pools above Shefford; great Kennet trout which somehow managed to sidle their way up into the higher reaches to spawn.

Before water extraction threatened the life of the

river, it must have been a stream of perfect proportions. Nowhere was it too deep and sluggish, but throughout its length, when the springs broke in February, it went brimming through the water meadows. Every year, unless the preceding winter had been phenomenally dry, there would be a fine flush of water in the spring to clear aside the silt and freshen up the river bed. My river keeper can remember autumn days driving his horse and harrow through the whole length of my stretch, loosening the silt and aerating the gravel for spawning purposes. Nowadays there are, alas, no horses available in the countryside for jaunts like this, and the gravel has become impacted with silt so that the river bottom is as hard as an Australian cricket pitch, and the fish are unable to make their redds. We partially overcome this by raking over the likely spawning places in the autumn, and fish do set about their family building with a will.

I wonder, though, how much spawning has been affected by the diminished flow of water and the silting of the gravel? Certainly when I first came to this stretch of river, about twelve years ago, there were many more small fish to be seen. In every pocket in the weeds you would find a plump half-pounder or two, lovely pale coloured, wild fish, and Frank Sawyer told me that, in his judgment, the river should hold at least four thousand trout of varying sizes for every mile. Today the river is shallower and slower, and the trout are therefore easier prey for predators. We are plagued by herons, those lovely but destructive birds, and wild duck come planing in to the wider reaches, to rootle up the weed and take their toll of every living thing from spawn to trout fry.

The worst of all, to my mind, are the swans who regard the Lambourn as a quiet and peaceful place in which to bring up their families. They also regard the banks as capital nesting places, and are prepared to defend them against all comers. Swans are too large for the Lambourn, and too pugnacious. They bring out the coward in us all. I would not complain if they were in proportion to the river. On the broad and powerful Kennet they fit in as dabchicks do on the Lambourn. On the little river, however, they can easily ruin half-a-day's fishing for you. Their glare seems to me not so much inquisitive as baleful, and as they steam over the very place where a big trout was rising, you can almost hear the parent birds saying to the cygnets, 'That's it, my dears, whenever you see a fisherman make as much a nuisance of yourselves as you possibly can.' Swans are beautiful creatures, no doubt, but I profoundly wish that the swan-uppers would come and remove all mine to their swanneries.

Then there are those small pestilences, the dabchicks, the moorhens, and the kingfishers, those flashes of blue fire, but they are so much a part of the river scene that I cannot be severe on them. But here I am making a list of nuisances on my stream as if the angler's life were one of perpetual irritation. He is provoked, of course. He is provoked, but he has to be something of a philosopher, and he knows that fishing – game fishing at least, is a series of minor irritations, illuminated by moments of golden glory.

If he did not know this, if he did not reach out after his moments of glory, he would never persevere enough to fight his way through the early stages and become an obsessed man. There are times, of course, when he says to himself, 'I will have no more of this folly,' and is on the verge of hurling all his equipment into the river in a final gesture. He is, however, out there again next day, with hope triumphing strongly over experience.

If we are to surmount these frustrating and often humiliating experiences, it is better that we should start fly-fishing while we still have the resilience and the unquenchable optimism of youth. There are, however, exceptions to this rule. An eminent publisher friend of mine had never handled a rod before we went together to see whether he could catch a trout in the may-fly fortnight. He was then fifty years old, a scandalously late age for anyone to take up fishing, but he was a man of great firmness of character. After patiently listening to some rudimentary explanation of the mechanics of casting, he attempted to put his may-fly over a rising trout, and miraculously succeeded at the first attempt. The trout, which was a good one, obligingly took the fly and turned downwards. My friend, excited beyond measure by this dramatic happening, struck as if he meant to hurl the fish backwards over his head. This was too much even for the stoutest 2x cast which broke with a twang and reduced my friend to tears. Now he might have given up at that precise moment, or indeed at any moment during the next three days, for not once did another trout rise to his may-fly. Even so, he persisted, and became a very fine fly fisherman and now angling has claimed him completely and he lives in a charming house on a delightful river with the utmost contentment.

I wish all anglers' tales ended so happily, and all the ones that I know almost always do. If there are other tales with sad and sombre endings, I do not know of them nor do I wish to hear them. Angling, with its quota of disappointments, adds up to the happiest of pastimes, and fortunate is the man who has an angler for a father and has, therefore, started at an early age along the road to true delight. I was indeed fortunate in this way, for my father was a dedicated fisherman, and somehow, wherever we went, fishing rods accompanied us.

I can remember most vividly every incident in a day sixty years ago when we caught dozens of tiny roach in a Norfolk farm pond. I can remember vividly too the surprise and shock of seeing a salmon rise like a porpoise alongside my father's trout fly on the River Conway. Then there were three dace coming up gleaming, silvery in an eddy on the flooded Thames near Hampton Court, and the barbel which went jagging and pounding away in a mill pool on the Ouse. There were chub taken on a big Zulu from under the willows at St Neots, taken, moreover, from an open Canadian canoe which was almost towed about by the fish, and my first trout caught in an overgrown brook which ran down from a private lake near Guildford in Surrey.

These fish, for some strange reason, have influenced my life. They have symbolized for me, even in the darkest days, a way of living beyond the market place. Escapism, did you say? It may be so, but what is wrong with escapism when it leads us to the water meadows? It has led me, at all events, to my small, square house by the Lambourn and I have no complaints about that. To live by a river is, for an angler, a completion and a fulfilment. Always, since I caught that first tiny roach in a Norfolk pond, always the mystery of angling has held me in thrall. Fishing is an integration with the springs and origins of human existence. It takes us back into pre-history to shake hands with the cave man.

V

Interlude in France

I THINK I particularly realized a sense of the eternal in angling one hot September day in France, on the River Charente near Angoulême. I was staying at a riverside inn, and the landlord's brother, an angler of note locally, offered to take me out for a day after the tench. The Charente, he told me, was famous for its tench, and undoubtedly we should fill a large sack with our catch. He took me to a wood through which the river ran, and where we found that a clearing had been made in order that anglers might come close to the water. The river flowed steadily and slowly, so slowly that it was difficult to detect any movement. It was deep, at least fifteen feet right in at the water's edge. It was clear and green, and down below us we could see, patrolling in an endless series of circles, the dark shadows which were clearly tench, and large tench at that. Undoubtedly, I thought, my friend was right. We shall catch many tench, and big ones.

We baited with brandlings, threw out our lines, and waited while our quill floats gently settled till only the red tips were showing. We, in turn, settled back in our folding chairs and watched our floats with keen concentration. We watched with optimism also, for we knew the fish were there, and that brandlings were their favourite food on this stretch of the Charente. Nothing stirred except that occasionally there was a tiny tap on our floats as if a cruising tench had touched the line with his tail. As time went by without success I asked my companion whether we should change our tactics or our bait. 'Monsieur,' he replied, 'one cannot interfere with destiny. If we are to catch these tench, we shall catch them, never fear. To change is to waste time. It is also to show ourselves as unbelievers.' He then returned to his contemplation, and we were enfolded in an absolute silence.

Hour after hour went by and, except for an interlude for a bottle of wine, we watched our motionless floats. At last, as the shadows grew longer and the sun began to sink towards the horizon, my friend stood up and shook himself. 'I am sorry, monsieur,' he said, 'that my tench have treated us with such disdain, but that is fishing, is it not? If the fish neglect us, that is the way things are planned. We may not have caught tench, but if fishing were not so unpredictable, it would not be worthwhile. As it is, we have stolen a day of quietude in a noisy world, and all through these peaceful hours we have been plugged into eternity.' He pointed to our floats and lines. 'These,' he said, 'are our connections with the unseen forces of nature. Even if we do not catch fish, they link us to a larger life.' This charming French philosopher was a happy man. He was not a Richard Walker or he would have caught more tench. Even so, even if he had sometimes to plunge into the workaday world, always he had his re-entry through his rod and line in that jade-green water.

Not long afterwards I met a different kind of angler on the River Loire. I was fishing unsuccessfully for roach from a moored punt when I heard a shout from an angler similarly moored some fifty yards downstream. 'Come here!' he shouted. 'Untie your boat and drift down to me.' This I did, and when, after some manœuvring, I came alongside, the fisherman made my boat fast to his and helped me to manage the perilous journey from one to the other. He was a robust, elderly man and introduced himself to me as a retired police inspector of the Sûreté in Paris, a sort of Maigret of the Loire, who told me that he recognized me as a foreigner from my fishing tackle and was anxious to prove that his river could really produce fish. He had, moreover, a large keg of cider with him.

For a time I was content to watch him fishing, using a long, bamboo rod rather like a roach pole, with the line attached to its top ring by a piece of elastic. The river there was deep and slow-moving, and from time to time the inspector threw in handfuls of cloud ground bait. He was using a single maggot for hook bait, and every slow swim down his float would flicker or turn sideways and he would catch a small roach or dace. He fished with great concentration, and his striking was extremely fast, and all went well until suddenly his float disappeared in a flash and he was into something much larger than he had touched before. He gave a shout of triumph and said, 'This is the one – the big chevenne. I shall make him into quennelles.' But at that moment he held too hard and his nylon line broke above the float.

We could see the float bobbing away downstream, and for a moment or two he considered whether we should up-anchor and pursue it. He watched it dejectedly for a while, and then, 'Ah well,' he said, 'it's like crime. The little criminals are easy to catch but the big ones break away. It is strange, is it not, but even I from the Sûreté could not arrest that one!' This was philosophy of a different kind, and I am glad that my friend, by the end of the day, had enough small fish for a fritture. I helped him to eat it at the local inn that evening, and quite excellent it was.

Fishing in France is always apt to produce the unexpected. My wife and I were fishing one day on a stream which runs into the Dordogne near Beynac, a stream which, we were assured, held many and fine trout. We found it to be woefully overgrown and devoid, as far as we could see, of fish of any kind. My wife, however, is a determined person, and towards the end of a long and empty-handed day she found a fish moving between two bushes. She managed to find a narrow gap through which she could push her fly and, after some misadventures in that very difficult place, she rose and caught her fish. It turned out to be a twelve-inch chub in rather poor condition, and it was the only fish we had between us that day. Indeed, it was the only fish we saw in that famous trout stream.

On this occasion our French friends had shown us not only philosophy, but optimism also of a rare order. In the evening when we returned to our inn and produced our little chub, the proprietor said, 'We had hoped, monsieur, that you would supply us with trout for our guests. But even so, with this small chevenne, our cat will benefit; and is not the happiness of one cat more important than the greed of many human beings?'

On our way home from the Dordogne, we came across a little inn on the banks of a river which was renowned for its good fishing. Preliminary reconnaissance showed that the best way of approaching the chub which we could see lying under the willows, as we looked down from the bridge, was by floating a large coch-y-bondhu fly down under the branches which overhung the slow stream. This worked well, for drifting in mid-stream in a fishing punt we managed to put a fly, now and again, under the branches, and every time we did that a sizeable chub would loom up and take it. The villagers gathered in groups to watch the mad Englishman using the 'mouche flottant', a method which they had never seen before, since their fishing was done mainly by dapping grasshoppers into small gaps between the trees.

As it happened, I was after bigger game than that, for during a prolonged drift I had noticed what appeared to be a small lagoon surrounded by reeds, through which ran the gentle currents of a side-stream. When very quietly I prospected, I saw dark shapes hovering in the current, and it seemed to me that a dawn sortie against these fish might well be profitable.

Next morning, therefore, at first light I slid out in my punt and, with extreme caution, moored it in the reeds at the head of the lagoon, which was nowhere more than three feet in depth. I used a tiny, quill float and brandlings for bait, and gently trotted my tackle down the stream. On my first swim down, the float had travelled undisturbed for some thirty yards before suddenly it checked and slid under. I struck at once and found myself into something powerful, something which, after much anxious playing, I managed to net out. It was a barbel of six-and-a-quarter pounds, a fine, well-nourished fish, but not big as barbel go.

When I came back to the inn for breakfast, I had four more barbel and two roach of a size quite unusual in France, where they run small, about three to the pound; and, awaiting me was a small reception committee, headed by the patron himself who greeted me with a kiss on both cheeks. 'But this is magnificent!' said the patron. 'We must celebrate this great catch. Tonight we shall have a barbel feast, and I, myself, will garnish it, and the mayor will be our guest of honour.' And so it was, but whether because of the mayor's splendid speech or the admirable Chablis which we drank, or the sauce prepared by the patron, I do not know, but somehow I gained the impression that the barbel, properly cooked, was a master fish. On reflection, I think it was perhaps the sauce.

These junketings were very agreeable and, as the mayor said, before the evening became too confused: 'Tonight we celebrate three things – the art of the angler, the skill of the *cordon bleu,* and the prodigality of the rivers of France.' This was a brave tribute, though on this occasion the art of the angler had not been particularly noteworthy, and the prodigality of France's rivers is not so evident as it used to be.

The French, in their wisdom, generally hunt for the pot. As Charles Ritz once told me, few of them have heard of conservation as we understand it, nor do they replenish their stocks as intensively as we now do. There are a great many fishermen in France, and very skilful they are with their beautifully-made tackle, but most of them do not return any part of their catch, believing that nature will bountifully fill in the gaps. Nature, unfortunately, is not as prolific as that, and the head of fish in French rivers has dwindled accordingly. This, by the way, is possibly why even a modest bag is cause for celebration. We are disappointed when we fail to catch fish, whereas the Frenchman is surprised when he does.

This is not to say that fishing in France is not worthwhile. It is worthwhile, and it takes you to the

(*Photo: E. T. Atkinson*)

Ranunculus in flower on the Lambourn

(*Photo: E. T. Atkinson*)

Major Whately looking for a rainbow on his water at Hunt's Green.
They lie close under the willows on the far bank.

most remote and pleasant places. There are rivers in Normandy which rival the best of our chalk streams. It also introduces you, or so I have found it, to this race of fishing philosophers. This you may see exemplified next time you are in Paris, when you come across the patient figures on the quais; men, who will sit by the riverside watching their floats all day. I have been to Paris many times and always I go to pay my respects to these brave representatives of angling, but never have I seen a float dip or a fish come struggling to the landing net.

VI

The Blind Keeper

THESE digressions have led us a long way from the little river. This is not surprising, for only by comparison can we form any conclusion about the relative values of different stretches of water. If there were dozens of rivers like the Lambourn throughout the countryside, none of them would have any particular charm or fascination about them. In a sense though, every river is unique. To the uninitiated it may be merely a question of whether a river runs faster or slower; whether it is clear or cloudy; whether it contains coarse fish or trout. These are only factual differences, however, but over and above them every river has a personal quality of its own.

It may sound highfalutin to ascribe a personal quality to flowing water, but to those who have become involved with a river, that quality exists. It exists and gives us much of our enjoyment. It is hard to define, this quality, but those who have fished, let us say, the Lambourn, the Kennet and the Test, will know well enough what I mean and how the personality of each river differs. The Lambourn, to my mind, has a gay, light-hearted and sparkling quality about it and, from the moment you have put up your rod and tied on a Greenwell in early April, you are conscious of being gathered up into the kindly, loving life of the little river. You have the whole season before you, and you know that it can bring you nothing but happiness.

On some rivers, and particularly larger ones, like the Kennet or the Test, you are faced with a grim challenge, as if war had been declared between you and the large trout which will so severely test you. Some fishermen like to feel this challenge, but those who love the gentle Lambourn look for something less stark and formidable. They find their challenge in problems of fly and current and presentation; in concealment and applied observation.

I can well understand the fascination of the bigger river, and I grab every opportunity of fishing the Kennet or the Test at certain times of the year. There your rewards are great fish, but the river itself remains impersonal and never allows you the upper hand. On the Lambourn you feel moments of control, of possession; even, on red-letter days, and for brief periods, of mastery.

I always remember taking a very fine fisherman from a famous river to the bottom field of my stretch. He had never, I think, heard of the Lambourn, and as we approached it through a knee-deep marsh, I felt with every squelching footstep that he was rather sceptical. When we got through, two fish were moving under the far bank and my friend, rather nonchalantly, put his fly over them. They took and promptly dived for the nearest weed bed and one after the other smashed him to smithereens.

As my friend thoughtfully tied on a new point, I could see him gathering himself together. He had been shocked by this assault and battery, but now he was on his mettle. Suddenly he began treating the river with the greatest respect. He crept and crawled. He devised for each fish a complete and separate campaign. During the rest of that morning he only cast six times in all, but he had four trout in his basket averaging well over a pound. When he came back to the house for lunch, hot and muddy and in need of a drink, he said, 'I have never had to work so hard for my trout, but then I have never been so highly rewarded.' He had enjoyed days on other rivers where he had caught many more and much larger fish, but never had his problems been spread out so clearly before him as on this miniature chalk stream.

The Lambourn is a deceptive river. There are days, particularly in early spring, when the casual onlooker would think that there were no sizeable trout in the water at all. I have often wondered myself, walking along the banks before the season opens, whether there has not been some strange migration which has led all my fish down to the Kennet. And then, one kindly day, there is a hatch of dark olives, and everywhere you may see the rings of rising fish. They have been lurking under the banks during the winter, and in May sometimes I catch trout which are black from the tips of their noses to the dorsal fin and golden thereafter down to the tail; trout which have lain with their heads in rat holes and their tails over the golden gravel of the river.

It comes to us all at times, this suspicion that the river is empty of fish, but I think perhaps that we do not make quite enough allowance for natural hiding places. Very often the river carves out cavities under the banks, quite sizeable ones at that, and, for considerable stretches the banks are concave, with the verges overhanging by a foot or so. These hollowed-out shelters are wonderfully good cover for trout, and they lie there out of the main current and safe against most predators. This is a position of vantage, and whenever there is a hatch of any kind, or food drops in off the bank, the trout will sidle out to take up station and you can see them there quietly sipping away with the utmost confidence.

I remember once having a field some three hundred yards long electro-fished. Walking by the river before the fishing took place you might have said that there were twenty to thirty trout in the stretch. When the fishing was carried out, however, no less than three hundred and seventy-nine trout of various sizes came to the net.

All this may suggest to the unscrupulous that there are other ways of taking trout in the Lambourn than fly-fishing. There is, for example, guddling, as I have heard it called, though there are other and less friendly names to describe it.

Poaching is one of them. We do have poachers on the Lambourn, but I doubt whether they do much damage. The trout are not easily approached, and in the hatch holes rolls of barbed wire discourage the man who ledgers with a worm for bait. There are also the occasional gangs of young hooligans who destroy seats and noticeboards apparently for destruction's sake. These are blemishes we have to endure on most rivers in these crowded days, and the countryside, alas, produces its beatniks no less than the town. We are at the end of an era when it was difficult to get to remote waters and when the only poachers to be dealt with were local ones. Now we have to contend with people from the cities who keep their tackle in the boot of their cars and drop in on any tempting stretch of water they happen to see as they go driving on a Sunday afternoon. These representatives of this mobile age are very specious. When you come across them they are very apologetic and say, 'Oh, I am so sorry – I didn't know this was private fishing.' They then drive on to the next bit of water and try their luck again.

Perhaps there should be more incidents of a kind which happened recently when a powerful keeper found a poacher using float tackle on his best beat of trout water. When asked whether he had a permit to fish, the poacher became indignant and abusive.

Angrily he produced the old and familiar arguments, but just as he was shouting, 'and I didn't see any noticeboard – ', the keeper stumbled against him and pushed him head-over-heels into the river. 'Clumsy of me,' said the keeper, 'but there must be two of us who are blind this afternoon. You didn't see a noticeboard, and I didn't see you; and, what is more, I didn't expect to see anyone on this private stretch of water.' And with that the keeper pulled him out of the river and sent him drippingly on his way.

VII

Where Casting Counts

BUT let us not think of animosity anywhere near the little river. It is wholly out of character, though I will not pretend that every morning in a fishing day is free from vexation. There is, for example, the sort of day when, for some obscure reason, your fly keeps doubling back on a forward cast and catching in your leader. We may put this down to a tricky cross wind, but really the fault lies in our own casting. There is nothing more vexatious than this, and it leads to some really terrible tangles in fine nylon. It always happens to me, moreover, just as I have found a good fish rising within comfortable distance.

Then there are the mysterious days when, after losing fish after fish, we take the trouble to look at our hook to find that we have lost the barb. This is inexcusable, of course, but then most of us are fallible creatures. I say nothing of those shameful moments when the fly catches in the small of your back and you have to remove your coat and probably cut it out, so firmly does it attach itself. Terrible casting, I know, but it does happen to most of us at some time or another. No credible excuse can be invented for these misfortunes, and the only explanation is downright inefficiency.

Those who approach their casting scientifically should, in theory at all events, never suffer from these faults. The adherents of Charles Ritz's high-speed, high-line methods should never get caught up behind. But they do. I was once broadcasting a commentary on a day's may-fly fishing when the champion whose casting I was trying to describe got caught in a tree behind him. I am shocked to say that I was delighted. The great man was mortal after all.

Most of us do not try to analyse the mechanics of casting. We start with our fly rods when we are young, and we carry on as best we can, throwing a fly by instinct and habit. That there are natural casters, there is no doubt whatever. John Hamp, so much lamented, was one of them. I remember seeing him cast on the Kennet at Kintbury over the parapet of a stone bridge, across a field which jutted out into the river in an irregular promontory and beyond which, where the river turned left-handed, we could see the outward rings of a trout rising under the bank. The range was about twenty yards, and John Hamp rose and caught the fish, a two-pounder, with his first, most exquisite and beautifully judged cast. It was a perfect bit of fishing by a master.

Not far from that very spot and in the may-fly season, I saw another single cast, though the result was somewhat different. I had been sitting over a really big trout lying off some rushes in a bend in the river. It was one of those fish which are so big that you cannot desert them and I had been trying every trick I knew for about three hours when that great fly fisherman, the late Frank Fortey, came up behind me. I explained the situation to him and suggested that it was his turn to have a go. He watched the fish for some time, studying among other things the run of the current. The trout was rising steadily to the natural fly but, as I knew to my cost, would leave alone any artificial that I could produce. Fortey said, 'I think he might take a spent gnat, and I happen to have one on.' He crept into position on hands and knees and then, after lengthening line, put his spent gnat about three feet above the trout. There was an upheaval on the surface and a broad back showed for a moment, before the fish went down. Fortey tightened, but held a fraction too hard, and was conclusively broken.

In this moment of consternation, while we looked at one another forlornly, a tall, thin figure of a man rose slowly to its full height from behind a clump of bushes where it had been taking cover. 'Oh, Lord!' said the figure. 'Oh, Lord! Oh, Lord!' and then, without further comment, turned and went sadly away.

This was the club's oldest member, and we subsequently discovered that he had been sitting over that fish for four days, and not once had it shown the slightest interest in any of his offerings.

Now why, do you suppose, had that trout succumbed to Fortey's fly after resisting every imitation, with spent gnats among them, which had been proffered to him during those four-and-a-half days? It may be that there was something in the size or setting of the hackles in this particular fly which gave it animation in the water, or it may have had something to do with colour. I think myself that it was largely a matter of presentation. Fortey cast the curve, for one thing, so that the fly preceded the nylon leader as it approached the fish. Then there was the delicacy of his casting, and the care he took over concealment. All these were factors, I am sure, but I cannot help feeling that there was something more. Many good fishermen can cast the curve accurately and put down their fly lightly on the water. Occasionally, however, we come across a man who adds some imponderable quality to his fishing.

Just as it is said of the successful gardener that he has 'green fingers', or of a great horseman that he has good hands, so there should be a label for the fishing wizard. There is a touch of wizardry in the sense that some supernatural percipience appears to play a part in their successes. It is not a flamboyant quality, and I daresay it could be analysed in terms of visual co-ordination and muscle control. It is there, though, whatever it may be, and we can see it in the performances of men like Sir Donald Bradman, the cricketer, and Jim Clark, the racing driver; in Arnold Palmer, the golfer, and Joe Davis, for so long the uncrowned king of snooker. And Davis, possibly the greatest champion of all in terms of sheer control technique, Joe Davis was practically blind in one eye.

We do not hear much of the great practitioners of game fishing for it is an individualistic, do-it-yourself pastime as compared with the great spectator sports like football, cricket and boxing. In spite of this, there are certain men who have become widely known for their outstanding skill. There was G. S. Marryat, for example, generally recognized as the greatest dry fly fisherman of all. There was G. E. M. Skues, also blind in one eye, the prophet of nymph fishing in chalk streams. There were others – not many – who qualified for the title of master, and there are some alive today, which brings me to my point. Almost everywhere you go you will come across a man who is outstanding among local fishermen; a man who catches more trout in any condition of water than anyone else in the district. These are the unsung Bradmans and Palmers of the angling world, and I happily met one of them some years ago in the West country.

I was wading and fishing dry fly for the lively little trout of the River Barle. The fish were obliging enough and would take my fly explosively, but somehow I could not hook them. I may have been too late or too quick on the strike, but, whatever it was, my basket was empty, until I heard a voice behind me. I looked round and saw an elderly man who had waded into the river in his ordinary clothes to give me a helping hand. He asked if he might use my tackle and then, casting with beautiful rhythm, and ease, he proceeded to take fish after fish. 'You see,' he said, in due course, 'it is really quite easy, but you must strike when you see them coming up halfway through the water on the way to take your fly, otherwise you will miss them every time.'

Now it was not only the precision of his placing of the fly and his striking which impressed me, but his water vision. I found that sometimes I caught the gleam of a fish turning on the fly, but often I saw nothing until the last moment of the take. He somehow saw through the not particularly clear water and timed his strike with the accuracy of a computer. Then, as he told me afterwards, he had been peering into that water for close on seventy years and he knew what to look for. There is something in that, of course, for water vision is of great importance and it can be improved by much hard practice. I am sure, though, that some men, for this particular purpose, have keener eyesight than others, and that all great fishers have the water vision of a heron.

I know a doctor on the Kennet, no longer young, who can see the trout's mouth open and close upon a nymph four feet below the surface. It is no wonder that he catches many big fish in places where the less gifted angler would say there were no fish at all. I remember being told by the cricketer Duleepsinhji, nephew of the famous Ranjitsinhji, that there was no need for him to watch the slow bowler's hand in order to detect which way the ball would turn because he could see the ball spinning as it came to him through the air. Such eyesight is phenomenal, but great fly fishers have it in the same degree, and their performances are phenomenal also.

VIII

The Evening Rise

I THINK one of the most perfect bits of fishing I have ever seen took place on the Kennet at Denford. Dr Cecil Terry and I were taking our rods down after a somewhat abortive spell on the river when a fellow member came rushing over the bridge to report a good trout moving about ten yards below it. 'I've tried him,' he said, 'with everything I've got, but he won't look at an artificial. He is taking all the olives that pass down over him. I wish you'd have a go for him, doctor.' This was a real challenge, and Cecil Terry accepted it. He took his rod and made a circle through the meadow so that he came up right behind the fish and about twenty yards below him. He bent double as he approached the river, and took up a kneeling position.

For perhaps ten minutes he watched the fish. Then he tied on a small pale watery, and began lengthening line, keeping it in the air until the fish rose again. Immediately he shot another couple of yards and dropped the fly most delicately about four feet in front of the trout's nose. The fly drifted down with no drag, and up came the fish to take it very confidently so that Cecil Terry could tighten the moment it turned downwards. All was well and Terry wasted no time in playing the fish. After allowing it a couple of savage rushes, he applied full pressure and worked the fish back to the river's edge where he duly netted it. It was a brown trout, a beautiful, tawny fish with the typical small head and thick shoulders of Kennet trout, and it weighed three pounds seven ounces.

Now this was a good fish though not a particularly big one by Kennet standards, but it is worth recording because the fisherman gave such a flawless exhibition of all the basic principles. He took the greatest care not to be seen by the fish, and he waited till he had made absolutely certain of its exact position. He did not, as some of us do, flog the water with the impatient cast which lands somewhere near the fish, near enough to scare him thoroughly. Cecil Terry took the greatest pains to see that his first cast was absolutely accurate, and that is where I believe some of us are apt to go astray.

The sight of a big fish rising steadily is apt to unnerve us. In our anxiety to get at him, we are apt to

(*Photo: Jasmine Marshall*)

'Worth trying a Caperer, d'you think?' The author on the River Suir in Ireland

Nearly ready for the net (Photos: E. T. Atkins

A difficult corner on the Lambourn

forget that, with every cast, our chances grow less. This conflicts, I know, with Charles Ritz's theory of speed of attack. Ritz, indeed, argues that there is here the fundamental difference between English and French fly fishers. The Frenchman, according to Ritz, always tries to be as quick as possible in putting his fly over a rising fish, whereas the Englishman approaches the whole matter deliberately. I think, myself, that Ritz is arguing from his own fishing experience. It is perfectly sound when the angler is as fine a performer as Charles Ritz or any of his fishing friends. The first cast by any one of them is likely to be extremely precise, and therefore they can attack a fish the moment they have seen it rise, since they need no time for calculation before offering their fly. It may be true that the Englishman is more deliberate in his approach, and that, as a result, he may sometimes miss the trout's brief feeding spell. On the other hand, I think that for the average fisher time spent on careful reconnaissance is not time wasted. I would, in fact, go so far as to say that most of us would catch more fish if we were more deliberate in our approach to them. But then we have to consider the circumstances in which a man fishes.

For so many of us our fishing time is limited to a few weekends in the spring and the summer, and when we come to the water, having driven down hell for leather from London or some other city, we are anxious to be in action as soon as possible, and the whole tempo of our fishing is speeded up. It takes a day or two for a man to relax, and give every fish his due. The mood is much more likely to be, 'there's a fish – let's have at him'. On the whole it is, in my view, remarkable how well the weekend fisherman performs, considering that, for most of his time by the river, he is really out of practice. His muscles are slack and his co-ordinating faculties are out of tune. What is more, he is apt to tire, and find that his casting suffers accordingly.

This, mind you, almost suggests that the only object of fly-fishing is to catch fish. This is partially true of the weekend fisherman. For him the fish is a symbol of success, a proof that he has not been altogether wasting his time, and that his skill is not waning. This, I fancy for many of us, is a by-product. Of course we want to catch fish. That is the object of the exercise, and it would be merely sentimental to deny it. Anything less than that would be an example of the typical British attitude to games, the attitude which says, 'it doesn't matter what the result is as long as we have done our best'. This is an amiable foible, but it does not necessarily produce the best results.

I can sympathize with the old canard about the angler who is not interested in actually landing a fish, but merely in hooking him, so that he may feel he has solved the problem of how to deceive the trout, and when he has done that, hands his rod to the ghillie to let him bring the fish to shore. This, however, is in my view making too much of an intellectual pursuit of fishing. The true springs of action, I suggest, go somewhat deeper.

If we agree that catching fish is the main objective, as it must be, let us also agree that the full flavour of angling includes many other ingredients. The triumph over the situation is one of them, the overcoming of natural hazards such as bushes, trees and beds of weed. There is more satisfaction, I venture to say, in taking a good trout when you have to cast into the eye of a whistling east wind coming at you downstream than there is in rising and hooking a big fish in the evening when the wind has dropped and the river is still, and the fish have turned steadily and resolutely to their evening meal. Not that fish are easy to catch during the evening rise which, to my mind, is often a disappointing and tantalizing period. This was particularly evident one evening in July not long ago on the Test at Bossington.

It was a windless, calm evening after a hot day and, suddenly, at about nine o'clock, every fish in the river started to rise. The whole surface of the water, which until that moment had been as calm and unbroken as a mirror, was seething with trout. There were splashes from small fish and dimpling rises suggesting Leviathans. There were large trout showing in porpoise rolls and small ones leaping clear of the water. It would have been impossible to cast a fly anywhere without its being in view of a fish, and the trout seemed to be oblivious of any movement on the bank or any action by the angler. It was enough to send an angler into a frenzy of excitement. Never, in the thick of a may-fly hatch, or at any other time, have I seen so many fish apparently mad with hunger. The only problem it seemed, would be to pick out the large trout and avoid the small ones. It was not, alas!, as easy as that. There was no visible fly on the water –

no blue-winged olives or sherry spinners – and it was impossible to tell what the trout were taking. It must have been something very small but, though I tried everything I knew, I only caught one fish, a two-pound rainbow, on a Little Red Sedge.

This experience of the evening rise is by no means unusual, and I never go out after supper in any mood of optimism. It is usually possible on the Lambourn to pick up a fish or two on the sedge under the bank, but I never expect too great things however active the trout may be. It may merely be my incompetence or lack of observation which makes the evening rise, for me, a snare and a delusion, but most trout fishers would agree, I think, that the evening usually sends them home brooding morosely about sticks of dynamite. It has, at all events, led me to approach the evening rise with philosophical detachment.

There is no more beautiful time of day than the last hour or so when the white barn owl comes ghosting from the spinney, and the swallows make their last scimitar glances at the river. It is a time for recollection and relaxation, and if a big trout gulps down a sedge, that is a bonus which the persistent angler has richly deserved. But all this is perhaps an unwise generalization. It does no more than record the residue of experience down the years.

There are, of course, evenings when everything goes right, when blue-winged olives or skittering sedges bring to us perhaps unmerited rewards. We all, I am sure, recall times when we reached our limit in half-an-hour or so, or when, as we trudged home along the bank, we suddenly caught, out of the corner of our eye, a silver ring where a mighty trout was moving. We may even, with the last cast of the day, have hooked that trout and battled on with him into the darkness before we drew him over the net. The evening, beyond doubt, can bring us adventure, and reveal to us fish in stretches of water which we had neglected during the daytime. It is, however, an eerie time for fishing and always we are haunted by the fading light.

For my part, I prefer the early part of the day with its promise, when we can echo the poet and say to ourselves: 'Ah, never hurry now, for time's all sweet'. It would be better, perhaps, if we could more often obey that injunction instead of pressing on like schoolboys, anxious to see what is happening round the next bend of the river. The trouble is that, on the Lambourn, you tend to acquire favourite places and are anxious to get to them. These are places where you rose a large trout on your previous visit, or where the river runs in a particularly inviting way over the gravel by a bed of rushes, or where you did in fact, to your surprise, catch a good fish at the beginning of the season. They are, these places, the background of your dreams, and you find yourself revisiting them while you sit at your office desk when much more prosaic matters should be occupying your imagination.

IX

Fishing on the Avon

IT IS strange how thoughts of angling invade your workaday life, seeping into your mind like an incoming tide which stealthily fills up the runnels and rock pools of an empty shore. You discover, at lunchtime in the city, that you are turning, almost without conscious volition, towards your favourite fishing tackle shop; an expedition which is likely to lead to some wholly unnecessary extravagance. You had intended to pick up a few flies or a cast or two, but there, cunningly displayed, is that new rod which you saw your friend using with such skill last weekend.

There can be no harm, of course, in picking it up and handling it, but, before you really know what has happened, you are trying it with a reel on to test its balance, and making a satisfactory swish or two, to feel how it works in the hand. By then, of course, you are beyond recall. You know that your fishing would be incomplete without this marvellous new weapon, and, as the attendant enters it to your account, you feel a mixture of guilt and the wildest optimism.

You take the rod with you, naturally, and perhaps that evening you catch an earlier train homewards, so that you may try out this wonderful new possession. When you get home there is, as likely as not, a howling downstream wind which makes a mockery of all your casting.

Still, the rod is there. Your mind keeps returning to it during the television programme. You go to sleep thinking of it and planning when you will be able to use it. You believe that you have at last found the rod which will give you that extra yard or two with great ease. And there is always the glorious possibility that you may be right. This, and the tackle manufacturers must be glad of it, is the stuff of fishing.

There are, I think, two kinds of anglers. One sort, and I plead guilty to being one of them, is fascinated by new tackle and new rods in particular. The other sort scorn what they regard as new-fangled gadgets. Rods of hollow-built cane, or glass, or steel, they treat with disdain, and they continue to use the sturdy greenhearts which their fathers gave them forty years ago.

There is something to admire in this amiably reactionary attitude which argues that it is not the rod but the man behind the rod which matters. Here, undoubtedly, they have a point, and sometimes they also have a rod which gives it powerful support. One of the best fly fishers I know uses a forty-year-old Leonard rod which, when I first saw it, seemed heavy and cumbrous. As my friend points out, however, it is a marvellously supple weapon and it does do most of the work for you when you have mastered the rhythm of casting with it. It is the very antithesis of the typical, stiff, chalk stream rod, which was devised to handle a heavy line and deal with prevalent downstream winds. And, anyway, the proof of the pudding is in the eating, and my friend, though no longer young, casts with beautiful delicacy and covers a distance which I should never be able to achieve with the best of modern implements.

Despite this proof of the craftsman's skill of Leonard and also of the man who uses his products, I am inclined to think that we are apt to use rods which are too heavy for the tasks they have to perform. There are maybe drawbacks to the short, light rod, but fisherman's elbow and broken wrists are not among them and the heavy rod needs a heavy line to make it work, and that means a loss of delicacy in presentation. But there is nothing new in this. Theodore Gordon, the great American trout fisher, was arguing about it half a century ago, and, to my way of thinking, this is all part of the angler's delight. The truth is that, when we try out new equipment, we are not trying to find easier ways of catching fish, but rather ways of enabling us to carry out the basic principles of angling more competently. When all is said and done, why should we handicap ourselves unnecessarily through using clumsy and out-of-date tackle? I do not suggest that we should take to the American reel which, so I am told, hooks and plays fish automatically. That would be going too far, but short of that there are many developments in fishing tackle which reduce tiredness and improve performance without in any way diminishing the scope for the angler's personal skill. The floating line is one of them, and I use it with gratitude, not because it increases the odds against the trout, which it certainly does not do, but because it saves me the fiddling job of greasing my line probably more than once in the day and, what is more, it enables me to shoot a yard or two more line very smoothly. But then, I am one of the tackle makers' ideal clients, a man who will, like Jurgen, 'try any drink once'.

There are times, of course, when we use wholly inadequate tackle and, in consequence, fail miserably. Some years ago I regularly fished for the big Fordingbridge roach on the Hampshire Avon. Lovely fish they were, thick and deep with vividly red fins, and the big ones, two pounds and better, were by no means easy to catch.

There used to be a swim opposite the Greyhound Hotel garden where the river came round a corner and made a deep eddy under a hanging willow tree. The bottom was shelving gravel, and there it was always possible to pick up a good fish or two, and there I saw the grandfather of all roach. It appeared to be dying, this exceptional roach, as it swirled round on top of the eddy, lying on its side and giving an occasional, feeble flick of its tail. Now, I have seen many hundreds of big roach, and caught plenty of two pounds and better, up to nearly three pounds in weight, but this fish made pigmies of them all. It was, without doubt, a roach and no hybrid, and I will swear that it weighed four pounds and more, this giant of a fish. I had plenty of time to examine it, for it eddied round before me only just out of reach. I tried to get close enough to scoop it out in my landing net, but as I edged nearer, it turned and slipped down into the depths like a torpedoed battleship. I waited a long time for it to reappear, but I never saw it again, and my only consolation is that I know that four-pound roach exist, and that one day some lucky angler will startle himself and the rest of the angling world by catching one.

If a four-pound roach is to be taken, it may well be from the Hampshire Avon, which is pre-eminently a big fish river. It was at Fordingbridge that the record British pike of thirty-seven-and-a-half pounds was taken in a deep and sinister place called Spicknall's hole. And there was an eleven-and-a-half-pound trout caught by a ship's purser from Southampton which slithered out of the hands of the landlord of the local pub when he took it from the well of a punt to show it to guests, and the last we saw of it was a flicker of golden sides as the trout sank slowly into the deep water. What is more, I was once smashed four times in quick succession at the bottom of the Greyhound garden, and I can only suppose that the very large fish which broke me with such a thump were barbel, though, at that time, there was no record of barbel so high up the Avon.

I used to fish there with Fred Jefferis and his brother Bert, who would always say when he wished to emphasize a statement: 'As sure as I stand on English ground.' Bert was a master at handling a fishing punt, and boats took a deal of handling on that deceptively strong river. If you got into your punt and cast off from the railings at the bottom of the Greyhound garden, you might very well find yourself crashing into the arches of the town bridge fifty yards below before you had taken hold of a punt pole. Bert would take you out in the heaviest of flood water, somehow miraculously edging his way along the banks where the current was relatively slack and dropping you into swims which seemed unapproachable. The fishing punt, moreover, was heavy and clumsy to manœuvre especially when there were three fishermen aboard and lumps of concrete weighing a hundredweight each at both ends for mooring purposes. In those days we never used to worry about the possibility of accidents, but the Avon has drowned many people in its time.

If Bert was the master navigator, his brother, Fred, was almost as good and he was, moreover, a fishing genius. I remember one evening in the bar parlour when four crack match fishermen from the Midlands were telling us how they proposed to strip the river of fish in the morning. Fred was sitting quietly in a corner and I could see that he was growing a little impatient. Suddenly, he broke into the conversation and said: 'The landlord's twelve-year-old nephew is staying in the hotel this weekend, and he has never fished at all. Now, I am not a rich man, gentlemen, but I will wager this,' and he put down a ten-shilling note, 'that I will take this boy out in the morning and that he will catch more fish than all you four gentlemen put together.' The bet was taken and the boy caught forty-nine fish to the eleven which the matchmen took between them. Fred had the extra sense of a great fisherman. He knew where fish were to be found, and when they were feeding and, if he offered to take you out, you could be certain that you would catch many and big fish.

Fred was a tall, rather saturnine, uncommunicative man. One grey February day he appeared in the pub soon after breakfast and said that he thought we might try for a roach. That was a lot for Fred to say. It meant that conditions were dead right. 'Fine,' I said. 'When do we start?' 'Four o'clock this afternoon,' said Fred. 'Not a minute before. You can have a go yourself from the bank until then.' I did, and sure enough, the fish were on. I caught dace and chub and roach, trotting down an eddy near a bend in the river; nothing really big, but plenty of fish. The day was mild, the weather settled, the water temperature right, and there was just that necessary colour, that 'shade of mignonette beloved of the roach fisherman' in a river fining down after flood.

At four o'clock precisely, Fred came along the bank, carrying a large sack of ground bait. He led me up to a side stream where he kept his fishing punt, and very quietly we slid into the main river, dropping down the stream almost twenty yards to a tall bank of reeds. There, most gently, he lowered the heavy anchor weights so that we swung square across the stream, with one end of the punt tucked close into the reeds. A few yards behind us, swinging from the branch of a tree, hung a decomposing chicken, dropping maggots into the swim. Fred kneaded up his ground bait into balls the size of oranges. It looked like ordinary ground bait – stale bread and bran stiffened with clay to make it sink, and some broken egg shells in it – but when I asked Fred, in a respectful whisper, exactly what it contained, all he would say was: 'Ah! you didn't see me prepare it, did you? No – and what is more no one ever has and no one ever will.' He slipped in a couple of balls, adjusted my float to a depth of about three-and-a-half feet, and we were ready.

I had the usual Avon tackle – a heavy float carrying a dozen large shot – and the bait was a big bunch of lively maggots. The swim alongside the reed bed was out of the main stream, and extended some fifty yards before it came to an eddy at a bend of the river. There was no wind, and the surface of the water had that seductive, oily look which to me is always particularly promising. I suppose all roach anglers have an intuitive feeling about the appearance of a swim. That one seemed to me uncommonly attractive. The pace of the swim was steady, and through the cloudy water you could just make out the gravel bottom a yard or two from the punt. I confess that I was trembling with excitement when I lowered in my tackle and began the first trot down.

The float cocked well, with the quill tip just showing, and away it went gliding smoothly as I tapped out line. Five yards, ten yards, a flicker – a strike, and I was into the first fish, a good hard-fighting dace. 'Ah!' said Fred, 'working up on the ground bait – try them again.' Another swim, a more decided bite – the float dipped – strike, and the red fins of a pound roach gleaming in the water. 'That's better,' said Fred, as he slipped in another ball of ground bait, and so the fun began. For two hours every swim produced a bite, sometimes just a touch or an unnatural waver of the float, sometimes the determined and unmistakable dip of a good fish. At first the larger roach took towards the end of the swim, but, as dusk approached, the grandfathers joined in and fed close to the boat. Roach after roach we netted, beautiful fish, mostly well over the pound mark, sixty pounds of roach and five over two pounds, with chub of two-and-a-half pounds to three pounds every now and again to add variety.

They must have been ravenous, those fish, for however quiet you may keep, or carefully you may play your fish, you cannot avoid some noise and disturbance in so shallow a swim. And these Avon roach and chub fight hard in February. Strong, determined fish they are, used to battling with a powerful river. Nothing upset them that day, even when I pricked a fish, or when, as happened once, I held a shade too hard and was broken. Fred looked at me reproachfully on these occasions and clucked sadly to himself, but it made no difference. Still the float dipped every time until, reluctantly, I had to admit, in the gathering darkness, that I could see no more.

I shall always wonder why the fish went mad that evening. The conditions were perfect, it is true, but I have fished that swim many times since in apparently similar conditions with only moderate success. Without Fred Jefferis, alas, for he died before I could fish with him again and that, maybe, is the answer.

Fred on the Hampshire Avon was a great master. Very often he would slide his fishing punt silently into a shallow, weedy corner where fishing seemed impossible until he pointed out a streamy runnel, a few inches wide between the weeds, and there you would take fish while others, in the recognized swims, had empty baskets. Silence he demanded, with no unnecessary movements in the boat, and cover whenever possible, and the strike at the smallest hint of a bite or the faintest unnatural deviation of the float. And then, after all, there was his ground bait. Perhaps it was just ordinary ground bait. But we never saw him make it and we shall never know.

There is a fascination in coarse fishing as compelling as any to be found in fly-fishing for trout. I would say that those who catch big roach on public waters are just as skilful as those who take big trout on the Test. And often they fish very much finer than the dry fly man.

I always like the story of the nineteenth-century fisherman on his way to the Thames, walking through the silent London streets at three in the morning when he was apprehended and taken that same day before the magistrate. 'Now, you must admit,' said the magistrate, 'that it was suspicious to find you walking the streets at that time in the morning. Can you give us any valid explanation for your actions?' The man drew himself up, looked straight at the magistrate and replied: 'Sir, I am a roach fisher.' Whereupon he was immediately discharged without a stain upon his character. This, I think, shows a very proper regard for the coarse fish angler as a man of integrity and upright life. There is no doubt that, on the whole, with the exception of the occasional litter-lout, anglers are quiet, decent and good-natured men. The angler who is out all day, quite alone, must have some depth of character to sustain him. He must also have a bit of luck to carry him through the less productive phases of his angling life.

It is extraordinary how some people seem to attract fish to them while others would seem to drive fish away. Richard Walker, our contemporary Izaak Walton, said once in all modesty: 'I have plenty of days when I don't catch anything, but let it be a day when there is a broadcast to be made, or a picture story of some kind of fishing to be produced or, best of all, when someone says fish can't be caught, and, as sure as you are born, the only decent fish that is in the river on the feed will come and hook itself on my tackle.' And luck can run the other way, too.

I have so far been thinking mainly of the pleasure fisherman, a name almost contemptuously given to the vast crowd of men who go to the river, not for competition, but for restful recreation. They consider, and so do many others, that match fishing, with its strong and often financial attraction, is the

(*Photo: E. T. Atkinson*)

A struggle begins on the Kennet at Denford Bridge

(Photo: E. T. Atkins

A good trout on the Kennet near Hungerford

very antithesis of the quiet and unorganized fishing which they love so well.

There are those, however, who affect to look down upon the man who fishes for pleasure as rather eccentric, despite the fact that the pleasure fisherman greatly outnumbers his more business-like brother anyhow. There is, at all events, a great difference between them.

Match fishing has been called 'tiddler snatching', and with some reason, since it consists in trying to take the greatest weight of fish in a given time from a peg whose number is drawn from a hat, and that is apt to mean fishing very fine and catching as many very small fish as possible. It is, however, far more than mere snatching, and it can develop into an exhibition of lightning dexterity, with tiny roach being swung into the keep net from almost every swim. It is an exercise in speed and swift reactions, and the lightest Sheffield style tackle can be cast easily across most rivers to the shelter under the opposite bank.

I remember a match with 130 fishermen competing for a steelworkers' championship. It was held on the Thames near Oxford, and the individual winner was a young man who had found a shoal of bream halfway across the wide river. He was enjoying himself greatly, and so were the other competitors. They came from all parts of England and Wales, and whether they caught fish or not they were having a wonderful time. And afterwards, as a contrast, we all had supper in the stables at Blenheim, before going home in our coaches.

Now that was a glorious day for the steelworkers, and an enlarging experience for those who merely watched. And if fishing can produce such days of agreeable relaxation, built round the severity of match-fishing, I have no cause for complaint. It gives the lie to those who sneer at the men they see strung along a river bank.

They sometimes look mournful, these fishermen, in their long, drab rows, but I assure the mocker that they have an inner happiness which they would, perhaps, not analyse or admit. This happiness is difficult to define. It is a sense of release from the tyranny of machines; a sense of wonder at being able to extract fish from these overworked rivers and canals; a sense of return to the living universe instead of being trapped in a fabricated hell.

While, therefore, it is not merely the incentive of competition which holds people, money does come into it, and competitors have been known to go home a thousand pounds the richer. You will see bookies on the river bank doing brisk business, and when you see that you know that you are in a different world altogether.

I have a great admiration for the match-fishing cracks, men who will very rarely be water-licked, though sometimes in hard-fished water the total bag is lamentably small. But they do not despair. They know how fishing luck runs, and next weekend you will find them there, concentrating ferociously on their flickering quill floats or their swing-tips, hoping against hope to strike it lucky.

They are remarkable people, these champions, and

very often their tackle is all of their own making, with the possible exception of the reel. And such tackle, too! Such paraphernalia for a day's fishing! You wonder whether they will ever be ready as they unpack their knap-sacks. First the tackle – rods and reels and winders and hooks and spools of nylon, and then, after putting up the huge umbrella which keeps the worst of England's weather away, settling themselves comfortably on to their baskets or their aluminium chairs.

Then comes the bait – tins of coloured maggots and loaves of bread and dust ground-bait and bran and a few biggish stones to make it sink if it is that sort of river, and everything put so readily to hand that not a movement is wasted.

It might be rewarding to ask a time-and-motion group to study them, though I am prepared to wager that the real cracks among them do not give an inch away or perpetuate a single wasteful movement. The preparation, the fineness of their tackle and its exceedingly skilful manipulation, all these things combine in a great match-fisher to keep him somewhere among the top ten in most competitions. They are oustanding performers, the champions, in a world of their own, and it ill becomes the rest of us to throw stones at them.

Their sport is a very spectacular form of fishing, and they acknowledge this. It is just the same with the trout fisher who insists on using the dry fly because he gets more pleasure – and sometimes more fish – and so excludes wet fly or nymph from his armoury.

The match-men do not like their fishing to be made too easy, since this tends to even things out, and their practised skills are largely wasted. Many of them, having fished in their Saturday or Sunday match, devote themselves to pleasure angling for the rest of their spare time. The fact is that most of these champions are highly competent pleasure anglers who found themselves attracted by the competition keenness, and entered the lists because they enjoy the challenge. But they like at times to watch a float without thinking that a silver cup may well depend upon its dipping.

For my part, I'm a pleasure angler first and foremost where coarse fish are concerned, and in particular I fish for the handsome roach, who is kind enough to inhabit some good water near my house. There was a time when I would rather catch a large roach than a trout, and I even joined a famous fishing society in order to be able to do so.

In a sense it became too easy. The roach were there – in the gravel runs between the weeds in summer – in the deeper holes and pools and eddies in the winter – and all you had to do was to keep out of sight and catch them.

The kind of roach angler I admire is Mr Albert Oldfield, who catches monster roach out of the public water on the Macclesfield Canal. But then Mr Oldfield is a passionate angler if ever there was one, and I cannot aspire to that. It needs some private alchemy to transmute the leaden qualities into gold, and thus to put so shining a face upon the world, a face that glows with satisfaction of catching large numbers of two-pound roach and over. And from the Macclesfield Canal.

Broadly speaking, however, my coarse fishing is indeed a pleasant pursuit, a studying to be quiet, a drowsy waiting, a satisfaction if the answer is right, and I do not like to be hurried over it. Just tell me that the roach are there, and somehow, some time I shall find them. And until I do, let me think my own thoughts in the silence.

X

Waterfalls and Tiger Fish

THERE was a somewhat stormy day on a Perthshire loch when a friend and I had been having a rather humiliating time with the Scottish trout. The fish were there, but the bitter north-east wind made them dour. The north-east wind it must have been, or the lack of fly, or our incompetent fishing or something wholly beyond the understanding of man – some vagary of nature that afflicts honest fishers on even the most promising of days. So humiliated were we, in fact, that we came in off the loch and left the terrible wind to its own sinister devices.

As we drove sadly homewards, past the head of

the loch, a sudden calm fell upon the water, and there, shattering as it were a sheet of glass and humping beneath the shining surface, were great trout moving everywhere. This was too much for my friend, who is an obsessed and passionate angler. In a moment he was out of the car and tackling up for his final onslaught, with the fish cavorting like mad clowns before him.

He approached the bank stealthily and began lengthening line when, without warning, and out of the bluest of skies, a black storm leapt upon him. It shrieked in his face and flung before it blinding rain and hail. The loch was whipped into white-capped waves, and every fish vanished into the depths. The evening was lost in a stygian nightmare.

My drenched and despondent friend crept back into the car. 'There you are,' he said. 'I knew it; a personal affront by nature. Personal, mark you, reserved especially for me. It always happens. I shall never catch those trout. We had better give them best before we are drowned by a water spout or struck by lightning.' We gave them best.

My friend left for the Cumberland Eden where he was going, under the best auspices, to catch a salmon. That, at least, was his plan. He rang me up next evening to report progress. 'I was into a good fish,' he said, 'but it went down a waterfall.'

It went down a waterfall. There, in that sad phrase the whole matter is summed up. There are many fishers for whom waterfalls are provided by a malevolent mother nature simply to snatch them back from the very brink of triumph.

My friend's angling life has been a series of unpredictable waterfalls. He caught his first salmon in 1931 and thought it rather easy. He has never caught one since, though he has pursued them in many parts of the world. Always the river was in perfect order the week before his arrival. Always it is full of taking fish the week after he has left. And if, by some exceptional chance, he catches nature nodding and some unalerted salmon takes his fly, invariably there is a waterfall to put him in his place.

There are two things that puzzle me about this unhappy story. The first is my friend's unquenchable optimism and his persistence in face of this elemental conspiracy. The other is the question of the effect of habits of mind upon fishing. Most trout anglers will tell you that confidence, which my poor friend lost long ago, is of the utmost importance, and that, if you believe in the virtue of a particular fly, however bedraggled and raffish it may be, it is more likely to take fish for you than the most perfect representation of the fly upon the water in which you have no trust. You infuse this certainty into your casting. You are not surprised when the trout rises to some monstrosity, and you tighten upon him with calm assurance even if he happens to be very big. There are, of course, a dozen hazards to be overcome before he is in the net, but the primary problem of deceiving him has been confidently accomplished.

For some of us, alas, confidence is apt to waver, and at the sight of a big neb emerging to take a mayfly, our knees begin to knock together. We need to acquire some of the resolute grasp of life possessed by that engaging, early nineteenth-century eccentric, Mr Twistleton-Fiennes. When Mr Fiennes was going out to dine one evening, his butler asked him if he had any instructions. 'Yes,' said Mr Fiennes, 'place two bottles of sherry beside my bed and call me the day after tomorrow.' Now I find that quite admirable. No uncertainty there. I can imagine Mr Fiennes saying to his ghillie one May morning: 'Leave me your box of mayflies and come back at six o'clock with a sack for the fish.' And the sack, of course, would not be large enough to hold them.

The truth is that success in angling is by no means a matter of technical skill alone. The great C. B. Fry, surely one of the most remarkable athletes of all time, decided at one period of his crowded life to take up game fishing. He approached it, as he did everything else, with the utmost confidence and the mind of a perfectionist. He broke down the art of casting into its basic principles, as he had done that of batsmanship, and I saw him demonstrate the theory with an umbrella in a Worcester hotel, when with a splendid Spey cast he swept two hideous vases off the mantelpiece. Minor mishaps of this kind did not deter him, and before long he was casting a fly prodigious distances.

To his somewhat pained surprise, however, he did not at once catch many trout. Indeed, he cast too well. His line flew out as straight as a ruler – a most beautiful sight – but, since there was no slack to be taken up by the intervening currents of the river, his fly was inevitably dragged away from the trout's nose in the most unnatural manner. That he overcame this problem, in due course, I do not doubt, but that he found it more difficult to put a fly deceptively over a trout than he did to make a hundred against the Australians, could be very stoutly maintained.

To those of us who do not habitually make hundreds against the Australians, or anyone else for that matter, this is perhaps slightly encouraging. It is all, as they say, in the mind. We do not need to have the superior physical co-ordination of a C. B. Fry or a Nureyev to succeed. The good trout fisher must have other qualities, not all of them necessarily wholly admirable.

He must, for example, have the cunning and craftiness of a train robber, and he must move as stealthily as any pickpocket. He must apply the results of close observation with clinical thoroughness. He must be endlessly patient. But if, and it is most unlikely, we possess all these qualities, we still need something more. We need, as I say, a bit of luck; a big bit of luck or, like my luckless friend, we shall all go down the waterfall together.

The incident which made me think of this happened at Carlsbreck, one of the lochs I am lucky enough to fish in Scotland, and they are to be found, by those who have permission, about half way between Perth and Stirling. Most years I go up there, thanks to my most kindly hosts, and start the season in April under the expert, the very expert guidance of Tom McNaughton, who was head-keeper for many years on the estate. He has retired now, but still comes out when there is fishing to be done.

Tom is a very good friend of mine, and I know he

will not take it amiss if I say that his benevolent instruction, and the fund of good stories that go with it, turn even a day when the trout are stubborn into a delight.

Tom, I suppose, is representative of the best kind of Scottish ghillie, apparently weatherproof and immune from aches, and a wonderful hand at disentangling tackle which has allowed the wind to turn it into a bird's-nest. He has a peculiar shake of the wrist which unravels the most awkward tangle, and a bundle to which I would take the knife becomes miraculously straightened out in Tom's hands. And in the meantime he tells kindly tales of all the characters who fished there in the past, and turns the delay into an interlude for laughter.

The upper of four lochs – Carlsbreck – is a large expanse of water, and holds big fish if you know where to look for them. Tom McNaughton knows, and gives you your chance. And if, in some moment of inattention, you fail to hook the trout which explodes at your dropper, Tom will merely cluck without malice. And if, by some happy co-ordination of hand and eye, you manage to get into a slightly bigger fish than usual, Tom will crow happily, not merely to himself, but to the surrounding landscape, 'It's a topper! It's a topper!'

He has the wonderful gift of enlarging everything, including your own happiness at being on the loch with him, and the hours pass very quickly when he is with you.

He is a naturally observant countryman, a sturdy, square, laughing red-faced man, dressed always in plus fours, and he is a remarkable ornithologist. He almost knows by a pet name each bird that comes circling over.

An April day, with a good ripple on the water, and the trout rising through the waves, and the curlew and the plover crying, and Tom to keep you company is as satisfactory an experience as you could wish for.

There is always something very fascinating about the ritual of getting ready to fish a loch. You thread your lightest line – at least I do – through the rings of your shortest rod – again my own practice, for I do not believe that the fish will necessarily be far from the boat – you tie on a leader and then some flies – a Butcher, let's say, and a Peter Ross and a Teal and Orange, and all the time you're taking a quiet look at the water and the possibility of a fish here and there. And miraculously, while you are finishing off your preliminary chores, the boat is packed with all your needs, including, best of all, a rubber seat and a flask of whisky, for beyond doubt it is going to be cold out there.

You may always reckon on a chilly wind, even on a summer day, and nothing except a trickle of water over the top of thigh waders, nothing can be more miserable than being cold in that kind of way. Incidentally, I know that this has been often said, but I repeat it here. It is wise not to wear thigh or any other kind of waders in boat fishing. If by mischance you fall in – and that is quite easy to do – your waders will fill with water and greatly hinder your efforts to escape.

Anyway, there is the preparation, and now for the fishing, with Tom rowing the boat diagonally across the surface weed until he picks up the line of drift, and you begin casting, at first blind, and then at the target of a rising fish.

You do your best to cover him as quickly as maybe with your team of flies, and sure enough he has risen to you, and you have him on, and he's fighting like a lively three-pounder in the South. When you get him in the boat he turns out to be just over the pound, and you regard him with great admiration. And so it goes throughout the day, with a break for luncheon and a dram for tea, and you may well rate it hard work, much harder than fishing a chalk stream, for except for the return to begin another drift you are casting all the time.

That is why I find that a seven-foot rod, with a number one line and a two-and-a-half-yard leader is restful and capable of handling three-pound trout and better, though I suspect that a minor catastrophe which overtook me on the Lambourn shortly afterwards must be ascribed to fishing with that splendid little seven-footer on Carlsbreck.

It happened like this. On Carlsbreck I hooked and eventually boated a trout of approximately three pounds, who fought like a five-pound sea trout. During the hair-raising battle he suddenly plunged away from the landing net, and went so fast and strongly under the boat that I had to put my rod straight down in the water and play him for a minute or two upside down, as it were. During that struggle I put a considerable strain on the rod, for I dare not let him run, and eventually I brought him safely in, to Tom's great joy.

I thought no more about it till shortly afterwards I was fishing one of Major Whately's pools on the Lambourn with the same rod, and I rose and hooked a large rainbow. I had him on for a minute or two, but suddenly I heard a crack and felt a slackening and looked up at my rod. In some mysterious way the top joint had snapped off cleanly just above the ferrule, slid down the line, knocked the hook out of the trout's mouth, and completely disappeared, never to be seen again. It must have been started on Carlsbreck and finished on the Lambourn, and it should have warned me of the danger of fishing too light.

That, however, it has not done, and I persevere with my seven-footer, perfectly repaired by the makers, Pezon et Michel, at Amboise. It is the ideal small rod, and certainly it is a boon when you take it out to fish a dry fly along the margins of the Upper Rhynd. There it is a matter of casting as accurately as you conveniently can, and putting your fly in the path of a cruising trout. You will see him rising and taking flies off the surface, and it is quite an exercise in self-control not to snatch it away from under his nose, but to wait until he turns and takes it down.

I find a small floating Skues' Little Red Sedge a deadly loch fly, with occasional jiggles to attract the trout. I know that the use of a dry fly is not widely practised or well thought of in Scotland, but there are occasions when this type of fishing can be murderously successful. But then this is leisurely, reflective fishing, compared to the vast Irish lochs, and Sheelin in particular.

On Loch Sheelin, so well cared for by the Irish Fisheries Trust, you fish for big trout, and during the may-fly season this is the way of it. You go out with a ghillie and an outboard motor, and you stalk the trout. They roam the lake, these trout, in shoals of five or six, and you start up your motor, and get within casting range. Then you put your flies in front of the shoal, and if one of these huge fish takes you there'll be the fight of a lifetime to come. And when I say big fish, I mean trout of five, six or seven pounds, and some even larger than that. In 1964 I saw fish of that size lying in the hall of a lake-side hotel, the bag of a few guests in one day's fishing, in a rather bad season.

Now this is all very exciting, and there is something about loch fishing which is most attractive. It is, mind you, a different kind of fishing, this stalking great fish in large lochs, and there is no doubt that skill and water lore come into it. The real loch-fisher who has spent every spare moment of his life trying to catch trout in Scotland or Ireland will know where fish are likely to be in a vast expanse of water – off the mouths of small burns, round the windward edge of the lochs or sulking in the depths – and he will adjust his tactics accordingly.

He will, if you care to check on it, generally catch more trout than the other fishers in the boat, and it is sometimes difficult to know why, since all would seem to be casting the same sort of distance with approximately the same speed of recovery. And all would be using the same sort of flies. There is, however, a difference about his fishing, a difference perhaps in speed and therefore a difference in depth, and small though this may be, it is enough to make the fish take his fly rather than others.

And he concentrates. That is a great and important quality which distinguishes the really passionate fisherman from the dilettante, the man whose interests diverge upon the other sights and sounds of the loch, the flight of wild geese, the beauty of the great expanse of sky, the whole superb panorama of loch and hillside, and the colour flooding across in sunshafts as the clouds scatter before the wind. The passionate fisherman is not sidetracked by these delights. He watches his fly and the surface of the loch heron-like, and always sees the rise, however much the wave on the water may make it hard to detect in time. And the rise to a wet fly near the surface on a loch is nothing like the comparatively leisurely take of a chalk-stream trout. It is a quick snatch more often or not, and unless you are concentrating you will inevitably see only the end of the disturbance on top of the water, or feel the farewell tug of a departing fish. You will then say to your ghillie, 'Coming short today, aren't they?' and continue to enjoy everything around you.

It is clear, I am afraid, that I do not come into the passionate category. I am only too ready to be distracted, and in a way this is easier on a loch than on a river. The loch is so vast and the possibility of extracting trout from it apparently so remote that you

Reflections on a river (*Photo: B. M. Marshall*)

More reflections near Boxford (*Photo: E. T. Atkinson*)

Where the left hand is useful on the Lambourn (Photos: E. T. Atkinso[n]

A pleasant ripple for loch fishing

allow your interest to spread over all you see, whereas on a river your concentration is more likely to be held by a rising and visible fish, and for the period of besieging him you are oblivious to everything round you. In between that fish and the next you may recline with your back against a tree and eat your sandwich, but if that peaceful interlude is disturbed by another obliging trout you will again devote your whole attention to him until you have either caught him or put him down.

Every fish in a river, moreover, provides you with new problems in approach and presentation, and there is no chance of losing interest or of bungling through inattention.

There are, of course, chances of catching something inordinately large in a loch, and that is satisfactory and may even take you into the lists of record fish, but generally speaking the monsters are only caught by trolling, a dull and inartistic method of fishing by trailing a line deep down behind your boat.

I would prefer to fish for the fingerling trout of a burn in Scotland, using a tiny rod and a dry fly, which you flick into every likely corner of every pool and run, and are lucky if you catch enough trout to make a fry for breakfast. That, to my mind, is the best kind of trouting, provided you can walk all day in waders, or move softly and barefooted up the stream. You need concentration for that kind of fishing right enough, for the small, greedy trout of the burns are voraciously hungry, and come at your fly like torpedo boats. And the old adage which says that he who keeps his fly on the water longest will catch most fish applies most appropriately to the fish in the mountain streams.

But before I was side-tracked into discussing loch fishing, and the operation of good fortune in an angler's life, I was saying that we are sometimes tempted to use inappropriate tackle with disastrous results. When I first fished the Hampshire Avon, I drove there from Manchester where a cricket Test Match had been rained off, and I began by using the sort of tackle which had done well in the Thames and on the Norfolk broads and in other relatively slow-moving rivers. This consisted of a small quill float and a couple of shot and a 5x cast. This could not have been less appropriate in a heavy, powerful river like the Avon and it was not until I realized that fine and far-off was not the right approach for Avon coarse fish that I began to have some slight success. I found this rather daunting until I took the advice of other anglers there and used a heavy float which would carry twelve shot and a bunch of maggots on a large hook. The problem on the Avon is to know where you may find fish and then to get your bait right down to them without having it swept upwards by the deceptively strong current.

I used singularly inappropriate tackle on one occasion on the River Suir in Ireland, near the village of Cahir. Lord Grey, in his delightful book, *Fly Fishing*, said that, as a dry-fly stream, the Suir was unquestionably the best in the British Isles. He added that it was incomparably the most difficult.

I was fishing a wonderful stretch belonging to

Colonel Charteris, and doing well in the may-fly period when one day I came across something which brought me up abruptly. Ahead of me, in a crystal-clear pool, I saw a trout which, at the most conservative estimate, must have weighed ten pounds. It was a beautiful, brown trout in perfect condition and, as I watched, another large fish swam slowly into the pool. This was a pike of about twelve pounds, and in a leisurely way it swam up to the trout and lay alongside it, occasionally giving it a kind of nudge. The two lay together for some time before a third fish joined them, a pike of about ten pounds which was immediately set upon and chased away by the trout's companion, who then resumed his station.

I do not know what biological urge was activating those two fish, but Owen Heavy, the water bailiff, was with me, and said that, in his view, it would be better if one or other, or preferably both of them could be taken out of the water. I sympathized with this. I would very much have liked to have removed the trout, but this was obviously going to be impossible with orthodox fly-fishing methods. Heavy considered this problem for some time and then, 'I have it,' he said. 'We'll use my medal.'

Upon his watch chain hung the silver medal of the local football club – obviously and rightly very much treasured – but at once he detached it from the chain and began rigging up a spinning tackle. It was inevitably a crude affair, but it might just be that, glinting in the water like a spoon, the medal could attract the attention of one or other of these fish. 'Throw it across,' said Heavy, 'and then be drawing it in front of their noses to see if the sight of it will make them take it.' This I did without much confidence, though anglers do believe in miracles, and at the first cast there was no movement by the two fish. I tried again; this time both of them lifted up towards the medal and then, with a convulsive heave, both fled into the weeds. Well, it had been worth a try. A ten-pound trout on a football medal would have been a little out of the ordinary. After that, I must admit, the catching of two-pound trout – and there were plenty of that size and larger – seemed rather a prosaic affair.

There was nothing prosaic about the barbel-like fish I caught in the River Medjerda, near Medjez-el-Bab, during the North African campaign. These I fished for on the principle that any river is a challenge to an angler, though the Medjerda was not particularly attractive. I was fishing with the aerial from a scout car, a length of twine, a hook which someone had managed to produce, and bread paste, and the river was yellow and forbidding after a heavy storm in the mountains. It was an act of faith which took me to the waterside, and a vindication of optimism when I felt a savage tug and managed to land the first of a number of evil-looking fish. They were, as we soon discovered, peculiarly inedible, which is why the local Arab residents left them severely alone. This, however, was child's play compared to a foray against the tiger fish of the Zambesi.

I had met the game warden at the Victoria Falls and had told him, incautiously, that I was fond of fishing. Out of the kindness of his heart, and I very much appreciated it, he offered to take me to a portion of the great river which, as far as he knew, had never been fished before. Stanley and Livingstone must have passed that way, and it gave me a very considerable respect for those dauntless explorers.

We had two Africans with us, and we loaded a boat into a Landrover and set off through the rain forests along by the Zambesi. After a considerable journey, we stopped and unloaded the boat, while I went down to the bank to look for a launching place. As I stood looking around in the reeds at the water's edge, the first of the hazards became evident. There was an explosion in the undergrowth, and a crocodile's tail thrashed round and missed me by inches. 'Ah,' said the game warden, 'I should have warned you about the crocs. That is the way they get their food, hiding in wait for man or beast and trying to knock them into the water where they can then drag them under a rock and eat them in peace.' I do not know whether the word 'peace' was the appropriate one to apply to that particular crocodile, but he slithered away and into deep water before the game warden could take a satisfactory shot at him.

After that truculent introduction, we were soon afloat, and were about to start fishing, using spinning tackle and metal spoons, when we saw, all around us, submerged except for their ugly snouts and eyes, a herd of hippopotami. They were regarding us with intense curiosity, and we left them because, so the game warden said, they have a playful habit of coming up under a boat and upsetting its occupants into the river. This combination of crocodiles and hippos was slightly distracting, and we moved on without undue delay.

The Zambesi, at that point, is an extremely wide, smoothly-flowing, clear river and before long we found a stretch which did not seem to be populated by any of the larger mammals. Here one of the Africans took the oars and kept us steady against the current while we began casting our spinning baits. It was not long before I had a strike and this very soon proved itself to be my first tiger fish. It fought with a sustained ferocity which was breath-taking. It leapt from the water, zigzagging here and there, went boring down deep in jagging, tearaway runs, and in general played like a sea trout twice its size.

It is hard to compare the fighting qualities of various fish; the plunging, thumping run of a big barbel; the first headlong dash of a carp; the ponderous dive of a chub for the tree roots; or the dizzy acrobatics of the sea trout, but I am quite certain that no fish in the world puts up a more dazzling performance than the tiger fish.

This was not a large one, but it was exceedingly lively, and as at last the game warden was knocking it on the head, he said: 'You have to be careful with these fellows. Only the other day, up near the Falls, a tiger fish slipped from the hands of a fisherman and fastened its teeth in the stomach of an African boy. It virtually tore his stomach out and he died later that day.' This gruesome story did not surprise me. The tiger fish is a handsome fellow, striped with vivid colours, but his rows of long, sharp teeth are formidable indeed. Magnificent fish, and we caught several more of them, but there were times during that day when I thought with particular affection of the Lambourn.

XI

River Portrait and Stocking

IT IS surely right that the little river, which carries with it such an air of ancient peace, should rise in a fold in the Downs where the archaeologists have found the remains of earliest man. Its source is in Lynch Wood near Lambourn where, said Charles Kingsley, 'the dead lie looking up to the bright, southern sun, among huge, black yews upon their knoll of white chalk above the ancient stream'. Not far away are the White Horse of Uffington and Wayland's Smithy, where King Alfred used the Blowing Stone to summon his men to battle, and, under the steep shoulder of Sparsholt Down, the

Seven Barrows mark the graves of prehistoric chieftains.

It is fitting that we should sometimes remember, perhaps when the trout are not rising, that our Stone Age ancestors stood on the very bank where we now stand, peering like us into the same river, and preparing traps for the fish which must have been an important part of their daily food. It is not difficult to imagine such things when only the water voles, the moor-hens, the dabchicks, the kingfishers, the herons and the swans keep us company, and nothing but the occasional thump of a jet fighter breaking the sound barrier reminds us of the paltry trappings of progress.

All up and down the river there are signs of man's earlier habitation – flint arrowheads, pottery, coins, and, at Bagnor, a dug-out canoe, and at Donnington, the bones of *Elephas primigenius* (the mammoth) – all these, and many more, show that through the ages there has been a parade of history along the Lambourn valley. Not only have the prehistoric beasts padded through its water meadows, hunted by Stone-Age man, but Cavaliers and Roundheads have fought for dominion over it and the unhappy ghost of Charles I still stumbles to defeat along its banks.

Now it is threatened by another kind of historical progress. The planners have their destructive eyes upon it. They will cut it in two, they say, with the roaring M.4 motorway, and I do not think it is because this invading road may come in sight of my house and across the best stretch of my river that I complain so strongly. I write in protest against the squandering of our countryside. The Lambourn is a small river running through a gentle and exquisitely perfect valley, and its perfection can so easily be flawed and lost for ever.

Already I have referred to the pumping station near the river's source, and the fact that after a dry winter the springs are emptied and the river is no more than a trickle as far down as Shefford. And now the Thames Conservancy propose to place nine bore holes – the experimental forerunners of many more – to extract water from the deep reservoirs beneath the chalk, and pump it into the river at the risk of exhausting the natural springs and turning the waterway into a characterless drain. They are well aware of these dangers, and doing their best to avoid them, but these are sad thoughts. However much we may try to cling to an outpost of peace in this age of progress and dizzily mounting birthrate, somehow it slips through our fingers. If our resistance is to be beaten down, there is only one answer, which is to enjoy to the utmost the treasures which still remain to us.

The Downs through which the river runs rise to six hundred feet and more. They are not like the Sussex Downs, bare and majestic, but benignly rounded, and criss-crossed with ancient roads, such as the Ridgeway and the Icknield Way. You may catch your first glimpse of the river as it flows through Lambourn and on towards Eastbury, so narrow that a robust man could jump across it. Right down to Shefford, indeed, it is little more than a brook, though great trout are often found stranded there in times of drought.

At Shefford a large spring comes in and immediately the river widens, flowing down through Weston and on to Welford, which means 'the ford by the willow'. There, in the muniment room at Welford Park, I have seen a map of the river, 'surveyed and drawed by John Garlicke 17 December 1725', which marks out the stretches, and they are long stretches, which belonged to William Archer, in the manors of Welford, Easton, Westbrook and Boxford. The course of the stream appears to have changed very little, though it was substantially broader in places, and would appear to have carried much more water.

What is particularly interesting about this map is that it was drawn specifically to mark out the fishing rights of several landowners, among then Lord Craven. The fishing, that is to say, was considered to be important over two hundred years ago, and I would dearly have liked to have seen Mr Archer enjoying an afternoon's fishing much as we do now and in precisely the same places. He would perhaps have worn a furry top-hat and a bottle-green, cut-away coat with leggings up to his knees, and no doubt he would have fished with a long rod and a blow line, using live may-flies for his dapping, but, whatever his methods, his enjoyment must have been akin to ours and conditioned by the same sights, and sounds, and smells. I do not know whether Mr Archer bred his own trout for re-stocking, but there are fish-ponds specially marked on his map at Welford Park, and it would seem that he took his fishing seriously. I often wonder what he would have thought of our ways of taking trout today, and sometimes I feel his kindly spirit near me, and take care not to hook his top-hat on my back cast.

It is at Weston and Welford that the river begins to develop its full stature. In Welford Park there is a fine, broad stretch, and just below it the river tumbles under a bridge on the Lambourn road and scours out a deep and swirling pool where big trout are to be found. Then it becomes a little secretive, hiding itself away among trees and curving into a length known as the Broadwater, where to rise and hook a trout under the far bank is, for many of us, something of an achievement. It requires casting a long line, with enough slack to delay drag, and the distance is just that uncomfortable yard or so too far. For me, at least, it is, though I have seen casters like Terry Thomas cover the distance with a seven-foot rod and a roll cast. Such performances, however, we may safely leave to the masters. The rest of us can cross the river at the iron hatches and fish the left-hand bank from sleepers fixed into the marshy soil. At the bottom of the Broadwater there is another sizeable pool, where my guests and I have been broken more than once by a very large, light coloured trout who takes with a ferocity which is literally smashing.

From there the river glides away among trees once more, a beautiful piece of trout water, though for some obscure reason, it holds relatively few fish. Perhaps it is because the sun rarely penetrates to the water and the insect life is sparse, but, whatever the reason, the facts are that the heavily wooded stretches of the river are not really productive. It is only when the river snakes round past a small copse and turns into a straight stretch, some two hundred yards long, that its population increases again. We know this portion as the Canal, and whatever the condition of the water, it always holds big fish.

One evening, fishing a Sedge, I was taken at the lower end of the Canal by a trout which was rising quietly under the left bank, a trout which in its first rush took me stumbling along the margin of the river and ripped out all my line and half my backing before it broke me on a plank bridge. What its size was, I will not attempt to guess, but the episode left Frank Fortey, who was fishing with me, trembling and speechless. If he had been able to give an opinion, he would have put that trout down, I think, at anywhere between five and seven pounds. And what puzzled and chastened me was that, with all my vaunted knowledge of my trout, I had not known that this monster was in residence, nor had I the faintest notion of where he could have come from so unexpectedly. He must have been a migrant interloper from the Kennet, but I have never seen him since. No doubt he passed on to one of the deeper pools and perhaps one day I shall have a more enduring glimpse of him.

Beyond the Canal, the Lambourn winds away across the fields to Boxford, where you may see it pouring through a mill race in the centre of the village. Just beyond this, at Hunt's Green, Major Whately has stocked for some years with big rainbows and proved that the Lambourn is one of the three rivers in England – the other two are the

Derbyshire Wye and the Dove – where the rainbow trout is known to breed.

The rainbow is a mysterious creature, or at least has acquired a reputation for eccentricity. In North America, where he came from, and New Zealand, where he grows to a great size, and provides glorious fishing, there is nothing but praise for him. He lives a shorter life than the brown trout, and grows much faster, and he is said not to like cold water, though the Lambourn is a cold river. His appetite is prodigious, and he spawns later than the brown trout, and that really is the sum of our knowledge about him, though theories are many. I used to be inclined to think that the rainbow is something of an alien in this small chalk stream, but, in my heart-of-hearts, I know that there is nothing more exciting than the first wild rush and the subsequent cavortings of one of these trout. They are not only beautiful fish, but they are encouraging fish. They rise conveniently when the brown trout are idling on the bottom. They fight like demons, and to land a two-and-a-half pound rainbow on 5x nylon in a weedy river is a triumph – minor perhaps, but a triumph none the less. Below Major Whately, there is Mr Billy Wallace's water which the Piscatorial Society used to rent, though it was lower down, nearer Newbury, that they carried out their extensive research into the question of stocking the river.

The Piscatorial experiments were interesting. When they first came to the Lambourn in 1902, they found that the trout were in poor condition. They were long, thin, black fish which were nicknamed

'Lambourn gas pipes'. They began by putting in two- and three-year-old fish and, over a considerable period, no improvement whatever was noticed. The number of 'Lambourn gas pipes' increased, however, and then the Piscatorials tried hand feeding unsizeable fish till they grew to eleven and twelve inches, but there was no improvement either in quality or quantity.

Then, in 1917, came the final experiment when no stocking of any kind was attempted. From an annual bag of three hundred and eighty fish the numbers rose in one year to eight hundred and twenty. They next turned a large number of fry into the river, and once more the bag increased and the condition of the fish improved. This confirmed two things – obvious, but sometimes overlooked – that we cannot expect a river to carry a larger population than its natural food warrants, and that substantial re-stocking of the Lambourn with larger fish is unlikely to be successful, and may even so upset the balance of nature that it does harm.

There are, I think, two courses open to owners of fishing on the Lambourn. The first is to put in large fish and then fish the river very hard, taking as many of the stew fish out as quickly as possible before they make too great a demand on the natural food. The second is not to stock at all but to do everything that can be done to improve spawning facilities. This entails raking and loosening the gravel during the autumn in places where spawning has been attempted in previous years but where, through the accumulation of silt, the gravel has become impacted and hard.

The choice between these two methods is quite simply one of individual preference. If you live in a city and make a long journey to fish at the weekend, you may well feel that the most important thing is that you should have a reasonable chance of catching big trout, and hungry trout at that, who have no especial preference for the fly they take. If your opportunities for fishing, however, are more frequent, I think you pass beyond the stage of wishing to catch trout at all costs. You will then find it more satisfactory to pit your wits against wild fish, even though they do not run so large. Mature Lambourn trout average somewhere between three-quarters-of-a-pound and a pound, with the occasional larger fish thrown in, and, on fine tackle, these trout will give you all the satisfaction you need.

I know that in taking this view I am behind the clock, and that rivers are now so hard fished that stocking is generally essential. I have in the past years stocked my stretch of the Lambourn with fine fish from Lancelot Peart at the Berkshire Trout Farm, but now the wild fish are enough for me.

XII

Fishing Diary

IT MIGHT perhaps illustrate the character of the Lambourn if we were to glance at some extracts from a fishing diary. They will not provide a story of gigantic fish, but rather they will be a record of an ordinary fisherman's tribulations, with an occasional triumph to lighten the darkness. My fishing diary is not a model one by any manner of means. I am too idle to record such important details as water temperature and so forth, and am more concerned with putting down facts which will recall happy or interesting days on the river when I look at them by a winter fireside.

I note that my first entry in that particular year was made on 1st April. It was perhaps appropriate for me to start on All Fools' Day, though the Lambourn is not an early river, and the fish are often not in full condition until May. Since I am always longing to get to the water, I comfort myself with J. W. Hill's admonition to start the season as early as possible. In that splendid book, *A Summer on the Test*, he says of April fishing: 'However bad your luck, nothing is wasted. The real season has not begun. All the best of the year is in front of you, and you have not used it up yet.' Merely to be by the river again with a rod in your hand is enough, though I note that on 1st April that year I did slightly better than that.

'Went to the Lambourn at Donnington for the opening day. Bright, with a cold, north-east wind – very unpropitious, but a trickle of olives at 11 a.m. and some fish moving. Opposite the bottom field, by the chicken run, something moved under water and then obligingly took a Greenwell; a rather thin fourteen-inch fish. Another twenty yards higher – Greenwell again – a fourteen-inch trout in better condition and then, in the faster water by Donnington Park, a fish nymphing a foot from the bank and cruising up and down a longish beat took the Greenwell and proved to be fifteen inches; a strong, dark fish but also thin. Another fourteen incher just above, and then a fish lying deep and shadowy darted up, snatched the fly and darted down again; a thirteen-inch grayling. An encouraging start to the season.'

Rather an over-promising start, in fact, for I see

noted on 3rd April: 'Another miserably cold day. Hard, frosty night. North-east wind strong. Little sun. Walked up Hollow Tree stretch of the Lambourn – grey and riffled – not a fish moved. An occasional trout showed under the bank but water must be very cold. No hatch of fly. Bubble line seemed to work in gusty headwind quite satisfactorily, but did not stay long.'

That seems to me a typical early season day though that wind must have been very bitter to drive me away from the river. Somehow, when it blows downstream from the north it brings with it a greyness which affects everything, and the river looks uncompromisingly hostile, if it is possible to say such a thing about so docile a stream.

It remained cold, and it was not until the seventh that I ventured out again, though the north-east wind was still blustery and savage. I caught one takeable trout on a Dark Olive, and three on a Gold Ribbed Hare's Ear. These were venturesome fish in the pool below the Hollow Tree.

The weather continued to be uncongenial, to put it mildly, throughout April. For example: 'Had an hour or so at Hollow Tree, but nothing moving. Whistling wind, very cold, no fly. Immensely threatening, black clouds: trees and farm buildings silhouetted against them in sunlight.' That was on April 9th, but it was a little milder next day. 'No wind. Milder. Trickle of fly. Fish slashing, but very pernickity. One feeding fish fourteen inches took Dunne's Dark Olive Spinner. Lost fly in another. Fished one-and-a-half hours for a one-and-a-half-pound trout which took every natural with a thump.

Rose him – a slashing rise – to Dunne's Dark Olive Spinner – but could not interest him again. Tried everything from Olives, Greenwells, Gold Ribbed Hare's Ear and Pheasant Tail to nymph. He continued to assimilate every natural with an almost terrifying bang. No sign of him moving or feeding underwater – just the explosion with the natural – no apparent drag. 5x cast, heavy, grey sky – must have been some light reflection of cast. Other fish also most reluctant. Took one seventeen-inch rainbow in Broadwater but it was painfully thin.'

If the Lambourn was uninviting under these weather conditions, the Kennet was far worse. Everything was depressing on a larger scale. I note that on 15th April: 'Went to Chamberhouse on the Kennet hoping for Grannom. Whistling north-west wind – occasional fly – Dark Olives – but no fish moved at all. Desolate and depressing scene. Downstream wind riffling dark and heavy river – countryside looking tired and battered and backward – gusts of almost gale force across surface of water. Waited doggedly until 1.45 p.m. – no sign of wind moderating or fly hatching, so to Donnington on the Lambourn and shelter, where a few fish were moving, one of which I managed to catch – one pound twelve ounces.'

I include these rather sombre descriptions of the river because I want to show a true picture, warts and all, and that must include the rough with the smooth. Fishing, in part at all events, is a matter of beating the weather, and I have no complaints. I merely report that, during the whole of that April, there was only one day which was sufficiently mellow to make it pleasant to be at the waterside, and I enjoyed my fishing in spite of the weather.

I see that on April 17th, in half a gale, I went down to the Hollow Tree beat on the Lambourn: 'Arrived just at the end of a dark olive hatch. Few fish slashing – one really big fish (three-and-a-half pounds?) leapt clear of the water, but the hatch was over and it was too late for attacking him. I carefully noted his position, however. While we were condoling with one another upon the conditions, a member of the Piscatorials told me the story of his four-pound trout at Kintbury last year – how after three hours, in which the trout moved only under water, he suddenly turned after a nondescript floating fly, followed for two feet downstream, all in full view of the angler, and took. Full marks to my fellow member for pertinacity. Thereafter, frustration – wind gusting through trees carrying cast into bank – two flies lost on tussocks as I fished for two trout rising close in. Rose and hooked on good trout – awkward cast round tree – felt heavy fish – but he slummocked off. Tired – casting upset by wind – pressing – timing wrong. So home, wondering whether I should ever catch another trout.'

The next day I went after that big trout. 'The wind had gone round more westerly and the conditions were not quite so severe. The wind was gusty and downstream when, at 11 a.m., I quietly took up position below the place where the big fish showed yesterday. One or two fish moved reluctantly, but there was no fly – the odd dark olive every half hour – the pool where I had stationed myself might have been devoid of fish. Perhaps it was. I remained heron-like for four hours – 11 a.m. to 3 p.m. – but no fly – no fish – absolutely dead river. By then, wind had strengthened – water was ruffled and unfriendly – it was cold under grey, rain-threatening skies. An abortive day – extraordinary that there was no hatch whatever. Always, hitherto, something has happened on this stretch of the Lambourn. Fishing is the most unpredictable sport, and sometimes the most aggravating.'

The next extract on 20th April tells much the same story though it adds that I heard the cuckoo for the first time that year. 'Next day I decided to have a change on a really beautiful, warm, quiet day – most exceptional – so I went to the Piscatorial water on the Itchen. I arrived at Durngate Mill at 11.50 a.m. (British Summer Time) reckoning that since this was 10.50 a.m. real time, I should just about catch the hatch, if any. As I opened the wooden gates to the car park above the mill and unloaded my gear, I saw a drove of dark olives careering down to the sluices. I grabbed rod, bag and net and set off up river as quickly as possible. Almost at once, in a scoured-out pool below the first bend, saw a really large trout cruising and picking off the olives, and wasted some ten minutes trying to cover him. I could not see him in the thick water, but he was popping up a yard, two yards, this way and that over a radius of some ten yards and it was hopeless trying to drop one above his nose. Cast a yard above his rise and he would appear simultaneously two yards to the right and so forth.'

'Gave him best and moved on to two promising bankers – but whether by lining or the natural end of hatch, both went down and the river became quiet. Caught a fifteen-inch fish on a Pheasant Tail. Saw a fine, deep, two-pounder come clear of water, and some occasional, underwater moves, but Nymphs were unavailing and no sign of Skues' "little brown wink". Keeper – on motor-bike – says phenomenal hatch started at 9.30 a.m.–8.30 a.m. real time – and trout glutted.'

This was a fascinating day though, at the time, it seemed rather frustrating. What, I asked myself, would Skues have done? This, after all, was the bit of the Itchen which he made famous. He would certainly have been on the water earlier for a start – but he might not have expected, as I certainly did not, that a heavy hatch of dark olives at 11.50 a.m., my time of arrival, was in fact the end of a hatch which started at 9.30 a.m. and that, therefore, the trout had fed royally and time was very short. Would Skues have wasted any time on the big cruiser? Possibly, if he had thought, as I did, that he had struck the beginning of the hatch and not the end. A big fish, after all, and in normal conditions at least a couple of hours to go – possibly more on such a day – would seem to be worth sticking at. My own failure was, I think, largely due to excitement, the first view this season of big fish steadily taking surface fly; a big and most promising hatch, and the possibility of great deeds. And so a fumbling, hasty attack, particularly on the two big bankers. The erroneous feeling that they were expendable, and that if I *did* line them and put them down, there would be others rising above – not enough attention to cover or the exact position of the fish – not enough care about the first cast – not enough calculation about the whole assault. Added to this, my nylon cast, originally tapered to 4x, but during windy spells being partly used up through cutting out wind knots so that it was short and about 3x; too short, in fact, and not fine enough – did not fall sufficiently delicately – remember Skues – 'Never sacrifice delicacy' – and while my casting was about tolerable most of the time, occasionally it was rather coarse, and the leader looked like a cable on the smooth water; and the trouble was that, realizing that the hatch was ending, I could not waste time to make up a new cast. This should have been done before setting out: a failure in preparation. At all events, by the time I finished with the cruiser and the two bankers, all was over, save for the occasional oncer. I have no doubt that Skues would have whipped out his limit quickly enough with a nymph, but it was a fascinating and baffling day, which made me feel that, due to hastiness and lack of preparation, I had bungled sadly.'

XIII

A New Rod

ON April 24th the cold wind and the grey skies were back again; dour weather which was redeemed by the sight of swallows for the first time this year. 'To Bagnor for a couple of hours, but nothing stirring – no fly at all. Then one of those encounters which lend so much variety to fishing.

'Very spry old man, walking briskly, stopped on Bagnor bridge and pointed to a cottage where he lived sixty years ago – "Benham House" – and spoke of his orchard, snowdrops, crocuses, daffodils and tulips under the apple trees. The river, he said, had not changed at all. Used to be stocked by Mr

Best (Old Snipey) of Donnington Hall – two tanks of trout from Scotland would be put in. Village boys would then drive the trout from the pool under the road bridge in Bagnor to the shallows downstream where they would pen fish against a plank and scoop them out. The old man's uncle, he told me, was a quack doctor – hair to his shoulders – fur cap – sold patent medicine in markets – drove round county in a fine gig. Summoned at Newbury for selling impure pills – made from rabbit droppings collected by boys – dried – damped – sprinkled with castor sugar. "And," said the old man, "my uncle got off – he beat 'em – why, what do rabbits eat? Grass, that's what, and there's nothing impure about that." His house, he said, was greatly changed – a wall gone and thatched barn, and all the trees in the orchard by the river, and the short-cut plank bridge. The village lads, he said, had to open all the gates for Old Snipey when he went riding. The lads used to shoot at trout – left white marks on them – an awful row about it there was, so he told me. A cheerful, vigorous old man who had walked out from Newbury to see his old home and would, of course, be walking back.'

On May 4th I went up to the Broadwater in the evening. 'Exquisitely still – brown, gold and pale green. Sedges hatching, trout moving quietly everywhere. Felt this was really the beginning of spring. The left bank miraculously golden with massed kingcups. Water voles were active and the wild duck came flighting in. Rose and hooked one big fish to black gnat. Thankful when he flopped off after great run and jump. Spent remainder of time drawing and watching. Three trout above hatches burrowing in weeds for nymphs or shrimp – one good fish, one pound and three-quarters or better lying in cushion of water between two sluice races, darting across current with immensely powerful wriggle into calm water under wall. One two-inch trout behaving exactly like his seniors, though he was chivvied whenever he ventured into their territory. Many grayling – some very large – two pounds and more – sinister, dark shapes sliding downstream with current – darting forward to take nymphs.'

I note that I used a Gold Ribbed Hare's Ear fairly consistently in April and the beginning of May. This fly is meant to represent, so they say, the dun emerging from the shuck, but I am afraid I am unorthodox enough to say that, for my part, if it does not closely resemble any natural fly, this does not bother the trout, who take it greedily. And if I find a taking fly, I stick to it, provided that it is something like the natural fly on the water in colouring and size, particularly size.

I note that the next day was very blustery again, the wind going south-west and driving fleece clouds before it. 'Broadwater 11.30 a.m. – black gnat again and some olives. Fish hooked above hatches yesterday, and brought to net on far side, back on his beat and rising like a clock. What instinct carried him – after being frightened and taken thirty yards at least from his little patch of gravel – what instinct carried him back to the exact gap in the weeds where I saw and rose and hooked him yesterday? The homing instinct of fish – Sammy, the three-pounder, back again in the exact holt where he was last year, though he must have moved up to spawn in the meanwhile. A big trout rose head and tail under the rushes across the river, tilting up very slightly to take surface fly, turning over – first dorsal fin – then, in slow motion, the big tail breaking surface. Watching this fish for some time makes it clear that we can afford to wait an appreciable time before striking – the upward tilt, the take and the turn of a big fish are so deliberate in water of a steady pace. A lot of trout showing, some of them obviously stock fish being chivvied by older residents – after lunch went down to Hollow Tree for tail end of black gnat fall – had one eleven-inch fish, rose two others but think I struck too soon. It is difficult to generalize about tightening on a fish, for sometimes it is obviously necessary to be quick. But, by and large, it probably pays to be too slow on average rather than too quick, since this should make sure of the larger fish. And we should watch our fly with such concentration that we can see the trout take it. Concentration is essential. This may seem obvious, but I fancy many of us relax, so that our muscular reactions are delayed and then jerky, while our observation falters and we strike hurriedly at a rise when we should tighten deliberately as part of a controlled combination of vision and response by hand and rod. Timing is the secret, as in most other things – but the timing of the great fisherman is calculated and exact, based upon observation and experience.'

The next day, Monday 12th, the blustery wind

had turned into a full south-west gale but there was a hatch of may-fly, apparently, at about 2 p.m. which went on until about 3.30 p.m. Flies were hatching in twos and threes, and the odd fish following suspiciously and slashing.

On the 13th I went for a change to the Hungerford Fishery on the Kennet. 'A beautiful day, little wind, not too much sun. Started at Denford Mill at 10.14 a.m. Nothing moving and no fly until I had worked my way up to Bracket Hatch, the main Kennet, where fish were rising to medium olives. They looked small. Presumably new stock fish. Took one of eleven inches, carefully returned. Difficult in thick water to see fish or estimate their size, but from then on – 11 a.m. approximately, trickle of fly, first olive and then black gnat on the water and fish taking. Most fish nymphing – but this is dry fly only water. Still, had bag limit to Lunn's Particular and Black Gnat. All, I think, round about the fourteen- to fifteen-inch mark – thick, exceptionally strong fish which fought exceedingly well. A thoroughly interesting and entertaining day.'

About this time, I had some difficulty with my casting. Although I did not know it, this was the beginning of the after-effects of an old rugger injury to my right arm. I note, for example, that on May 14th: 'Broke top joint of light rod, catching fly in tuft in gusty wind. Had always been conscious that it was stiff and unsympathetic, this rod, and that it made casting like using a rigid pole – possible, but hard work. Changed over to eight foot six, far more supple rod. Heavier, but somehow much easier in the hand, kindlier action, rod doing the work. To pool, where casting seemed much easier and striking effective. Three fish in tail of pool caught and returned – nothing stirring to may-fly in pool itself. Then to hatches – there saw biggish fish come up through sluices. Caught him – one-and-three-quarter pounds and rose Sammy, casting with relative ease under far bank. Action of rod appears to do the work: generally both accurate and delicate, though occasional heavy delivery.'

Next day I continued my rod experiment: 'fished up the whole of my stretch, from 10.30 a.m. to 5 p.m. Hardly any may-fly hatched, though at 5 p.m., on Broadwater, may-fly hatching and big fish moving everywhere. Must be silt which encourages the fly. Using eight-foot-six-inch more supple rod, my casting improved out of all knowledge as if a twelve handicap golfer had, overnight, become scratch. Had three good fish in most difficult place under chesnut trees overhanging water, and several more fish standing well back. The change is so startling that I can really hardly believe it and wonder if it was just an inspired day with everything functioning and co-ordinating perfectly – like a cricket innings when you see the ball as large as a football and brain and eye, hand and feet, all work instinctively together. Must reserve judgment till I have made further trials, but I hope profoundly that the change is real.'

The change was real, and ever since I have used more pliant rods. On looking back, it was strange how, for many years, I had accepted, without question, the theory that, for dry fly fishing on chalk streams, a stiff action was necessary in a rod in order to deal with downstream winds. I do not mean that I like a soft rod, but one which has firmness in it and yet is more pliable. This, I am sure, is the kind of action found by Skues in the W.B.R. – World's Best Rod – made by Leonard in America.

In the meanwhile the may-fly hatch was still on and on 19th May: 'I spent some time looking for my lost fly box which contained all my may-flies and when I had found it under a river-side seat, went in afternoon to Broadwater. Trout moving everywhere to may-fly. Fish rising in Sammy's place – covered him – rose and caught twelve-ounce fish – deputizing for Sammy as a food taster no doubt. Moved on to obviously good fish showing head and tail under far bank – caught him – fifteen inches but thin – should have been at least one-and-a-half pounds. Fish showing all the way up Broadwater, and steady hatch of fly, but nothing whatever above plank bridge in pool or top field. Back by road to Broadwater where hatch (5 p.m.) was thickest. Counted eighteen fish moving within one minute in casting distance. Caught beautifully conditioned and strong, wild fish at first cast – shook him off without handling and gave up fishing. It would have been murder.'

The may-fly hatch was almost confined to the Broadwater, and this has been true in every season. The Broadwater is covered with silt, which may-fly nymphs like, and this, I am sure, is the explanation. This Broadwater silt seems to produce fly when they are appearing nowhere else, and it makes me wonder whether the theory that we must have clean gravel everywhere can be generally applied.

Next day I went to Hungerford again: 'Dull, cool and strong, gusty wind directly downstream. Little fly – the odd fish rising, mostly nymphing. Some small fish to Gold Ribbed Hare's Ear, but mostly thrashed unhappily into exasperating wind – waiting for lulls, and then having line flopped on water over trout's head by sudden gust, or whipped into the sedges or smacked against the rod on back cast or knotted hideously – until decided that really, after a month of downstream winds fishing is a much overrated pastime, especially with so little moving and no sign of big fish. River not particularly attractive – heavy and swollen. Then all put right by amusing bit of fishing from the garden. Good trout moving steadily under bank near ash tree. Only way to approach by crawling and finally sitting behind rushes on bank and back-handing over them. Refused Greenwell – but finally, avoiding hazards of tree, bushes, nettles, rushes and wind, managed to put Black Spider over him, he took and was duly hooked and landed, after a deal of very savage head shaking. A fine conditioned, one-and-three-quarter-pound trout who saved the day.'

On May 21st there was: 'Howling wind again, of course. If this goes on throughout the Lambourn may-fly, it will mean no may-fly at all in two years' time – all the fly will be swept so far away from the river. Piscatorial keeper at Bagnor tells me he has seen no may-fly hatch whatever and this cold water is holding it back. But the Broadwater is cold too! To Broadwater in the afternoon from 2.15 to 4.30 p.m. May-fly hatching, but very few and irregularly with fish splashing at them as they were whisked off the surface by the wind. It looks as if the main Broadwater hatch is over.'

Then one of those abortive days which chasten us all: 'Half a gale again. To Hollow Tree, wind being southerly and therefore blustering upstream. May-fly hatching sporadically, some fish moving. Fished fairly well despite wild gusts, but still apt to be too quick on strike. Finally hooked big fish above lower boundary. Did not realize how big until he took out all my line down to the last foot of backing before plunging into weed bed in Saunderson's water. Two pounds and better – saw length of him as belly gleamed when he turned over. Hooked another good fish in rushes one hundred yards above boundary. Made no impression on him. Then hook came out. Rose and pricked big cruiser in pool above. Watched him rise, waited till he turned but still apparently too soon.' These days, I suppose, are good for our souls, and the margin between success and failure is so narrow that we cannot always expect things to go right. But to hook three big fish in one day and lose all of them through incompetence is chastening indeed.

Obviously, however, I was due for punishment and I notice on May 27th one of the really tantalizing and typical may-fly days. Apparently perfect conditions – warm, little wind, and when I arrived at Hollow Tree about 1.30 p.m.: 'Fish moving everywhere but obviously nymphing. No hatch yet, but I tried with submerged hackle fly, and within ten minutes had caught a twelve-inch fish and lost two others, one very big, through knots pulling out in nylon cast. A home-made cast, I hasten to say, and I must have been careless when I made it up. Still, there seemed the prospect of great things and soon I had a good thirteen-inch fish at the lower boundary, and lost another which kicked off; both to hackle fly awash in surface film. Then began frustration. Fly started to hatch. By 3.30 p.m. a very substantial hatch developed and fish were smashing at the natural round, often right at my feet, apparently taking no notice of me. It seemed that I should inevitably catch many fish. But for the two-hour duration of the hatch, hardly a fish would look at any of the dozen varieties of may-fly to 4x. And all I did was to prick two good fish to a Caperer, and catch one fourteen-inch fish, foul hooked after a smashing rise. Most baffling. Really big fish moving everywhere and I was casting no worse than usual. The rises were noisy and violent – possibly following nymph to surface. There could have been some quality in the light; thunder clouds developed, with that peculiar steely luminosity which intensifies the cast shadow.'

XIV

That Big Rainbow

THE chastening process continued next day when I see that: 'Another tantalizing may-fly day at Hollow Tree. Hatch started about 2.14 p.m. Good fish showed everywhere in splashing, explosive rises, sometimes to natural, sometimes underwater. I soon had a thirteen-and-a-half-inch fish to submerged hackle fly, and connected with several more but all of them floundered off. Fishing 4x, they would not look at any of the dozen varieties of floating fly, though I tried steadily rising fish assiduously. There must be some explanation, and at the root of it three possible causes occurred to me. (1) Light: again there were thunder clouds about and the steely light giving a sharp clarity to everything. River there runs west to east, and the sun, therefore, was roughly in my face and was throwing a shadow ahead of the fly and cast. The density of the artificial may-fly possibly was much greater than that of the natural and the fish would see floating towards it a heavy, dark mass in contrast to the diaphanous natural, however lightly dressed the artificial might be. (2) Using 4x nylon into a slight head wind, there was a tendency for the last bit of the cast, through the parachute effect of the heavy fly, to turn back on itself and present, if not exactly a bird's nest, at all events a loop or twist of nylon. This may have alerted the fish. (3) The combination of the first two possibilities put the fish on their guard and their explosive rises, therefore, were in fact snatches of scared fish making a quick grab though conscious of danger. This, and the fact that sometimes they were following may-fly nymphs to the surface. Often you would see a fly hatch as a fish boiled at it. There is some substantiation of the light theory in the fact that at 6 p.m., and as the sun dropped behind hilltop trees, fish began to rise more quietly and took an artificial in the normal way. I had two good fish in the last half-hour on spent fly, though this was further up river and in very awkward conditions with a cover of tall rushes and bank of trees directly behind me, again a new factor. The river is shallow and clear and cover is vital.'

The next day I went again to the Hollow Tree: 'It was still thundery but at 2.15 p.m. a good hatch of may-fly began and fish came well for the artificial. Had four fish to floating spent fly in an hour, all fourteen-inch or over.'

Then a fortnight or so of the may-fly on the Kennet at Kintbury, with its usual ups and downs, its disappointments and its compensating successes. It all came to a head on June 16th when Lancelot Peart most kindly asked me over for an evening on his stretch of the River Dunn.

'Hot and still. Clouds of fly along the Bath Road. At 6.30 p.m. fish were moving vigorously underwater, but would take no notice of any surface fly. There was a small hatch, and when the sun dropped behind the trees, about 8.30 p.m., the fish were on to spent fly, still very choosy and obviously cruising. There was one big fish under willows at the top of the stretch who occasionally took with a prodigious thump and was cart-wheeling under the surface. After fishing for him a long time with various patterns, eventually rose him to a big, spent fly and he took with a roll, and the solid plunge as I tightened on him showed that he was very large. He set off like a steam roller, and jumped twice with such a prodigious splash that he brought another angler running downstream to see what was happening, thinking that someone had fallen into the river. Next came a series of ferocious rushes and head shakings before he careered upstream above the railings at the top of Lancelot Peart's water, and under the willows where I could not follow him. With side strain I managed to turn him, though it seemed for a time that I should have no effect on him at all, and he only turned just when he appeared to be out of control. He came down, and plunged for a wooden board at the head of a small inlet, rubbing the line ominously against it, and I began walking him down, and finally, after much circling, and two shots with the net, brought him to dry land. A most perfectly proportioned rainbow weighing five pounds twelve ounces. A superb evening.' An episode like that makes up for all the disappointments and misfortunes of a difficult season but, before I become too pleased with myself or with my rainbow, I must record that seven days before, in the Kennet, Cecil Terry had taken a brown trout weighing seven pounds eight ounces. That gets matters into a proper perspective. My rainbow, after all, was not a particularly large respresentative of the species, though he was quite large enough for me.

The rest of that month was exceedingly hot and thundery. The Lambourn, moreover, was virtually choked by weed. I note: 'Ranunculus now a sea of snowy blossoms across top of Broadwater. Weeds heavy everywhere – water deep, held up by weed and trickling slowly in narrow runs between weed patches. Fish very shy. Notice they turn to follow the fly as it is retrieved below them going underwater. Vibration must suggest a swimming nymph.'

Then on June 30th I had: 'An amusing hour between torrential storms in Broadwater. One small fish at hatches returned – next fish lying in weeds, stimulated by dragging, sunk fly. Takes floater next cast – thirteen inches. Fish rising in fast run between weeds at something invisible refuses all floaters, though no apparent drag, but takes nymph just below surface, rising from bottom slowly – hooked – runs strongly and solidly into weed bed as skies open and a deluge, almost a cloudburst, cascades down. Retire from sleeper in rushes to bank – put rod down – put on plastic mac – pick up rod and find fish still there. Move upstream twenty yards – work fish free, persuading him over weeds and land him – fourteen inches, good condition.'

The excessively humid and sultry weather persisted well into July, and made fishing a matter of taking the odd trout out of pockets in the weed and waiting till late evening to start fishing at all. On July 12th I note that: 'Weed cutting has begun – patches of weed left but water level dropped by approximately a foot and great banks of silt revealed. One thirteen-inch trout to Pheasant Tail nymph at top of Broadwater. Trout follow nymph like sharks but grayling ignore it – possibly not deep enough. Grayling rootling out nymphs in gravel.'

Then, abruptly, the weather changed and we had gale-force winds and driving rain and chilly conditions. 'An October day with very occasional glimpses of sun – fishing out of the question. Reviewed Sawyer's new book, *Nymphs and the Trout* – very good and stimulating. Sawyer argues that nymph fishing should be regarded as an art in its own right rather than a subsidiary and minor branch of dry-fly fishing. He challenges heavy, tapered lines saying that they scare ninety-five per cent of trout. Of one hundred trout fished for, dry fly or nymph, Sawyer estimates that fifty are missed, twenty pricked, fifteen break on strike and ten are lost in weed. Only five out of every hundred landed. This, he argues, because heavy, tapered line creates craze for long casting beyond effective control. These figures are, in a sense, comforting.

'Fishing is a solitary sport, and it is difficult to compare your results with those of other anglers. I should say, however, that the estimate of only five out of every hundred trout fished for are in fact landed, is just about right of my own fishing. I do, perhaps, sometimes notch up a better percentage than I used to years ago, but that, quite simply, is because I no longer fish indiscriminately whenever I see a trout moving, but take time to estimate its size and weigh up the chances of catching it before I make my first cast. It would be interesting, though laborious, to keep a tally of trout fished for compared to trout caught throughout a season. I think many of us might be considerably surprised at the result. And the effect of missing ninety-five per cent, let us say, must be that ninety-five out of every hundred fish are pricked or put down or have a fly left in them. In general they become highly educated, and perhaps the surprising thing is that so many trout are caught.

XV

A Day with Frank Sawyer

ON July 24th I went to spend the day with river keeper Frank Sawyer, on the Upper Avon, calling for him at his home – a large, rambling, old thatched house where Sawyer has a small, sparsely furnished room where he writes – a typewriter on a tiny desk – a small bookcase full of angling books – periodicals like *The Field* and *Trout and Salmon* scattered about. Rods, guns, landing nets. Sawyer talks easily and naturally and with an almost biblical simplicity and choice of phrase. When we were looking at the clear, sparkling river he spoke of 'the living water' and conveyed his care and love for the river and all the life in and around it.

About herons he said that, provided there were not too many of them, they were such beautiful birds, so perfectly designed for their fishing, that he could not begrudge them a few trout. He watched them for hours fishing in the shallower reaches – their deliberate walk – one foot firmly and silently planted before the next one moved – head poised to strike – and he told me that in the feathers at the back of their neck they have a powder with which they clean the slime off their claws after they have taken a fish. He thought there was nothing in the theory that they have some sort of grease on their legs which attracts fish when they are standing in the river. The only river creatures that Sawyer dislikes are swans, and swans, he said, he positively hates. They were getting absolutely out of control, and as many as a hundred sometimes descended on his six-mile stretch.

Of fishes' sense of smell and taste, he said that they were very much stronger than we realized. When using the relatively new silicone fly floatants, he has proved, by experiment, that trout eject the fly much more quickly than with the old-fashioned oil preparation, and he makes his may-flies float with beef fat and finds that the trout hold on to it much longer than they do to the undressed fly.

He uses an eight-foot-ten-inch French rod which has his name inscribed upon it. It was designed and given to him by Charles Ritz, and he values it greatly. It is very light, very pliable, rather like the old greenheart wet fly rod but with a swift tip action which he considers essential for hooking on very fine casts. With it he uses a number one tapered line and casts most beautifully – picking the fly off and recasting with the roll action – flicking it easily across the river with trees solid behind him – always in close control with the left hand gathering in line to keep contact – striking with a sideways wrist flick. He has very powerful wrists and forearms. The nymphs he uses – tied in sizes from 00 to 1 – have no hackles or whisks, but tails and a heavy thorax and are dressed with very fine wire to help sinking. He pitches them so that they have an almost vertical entry and sink at once and he gives a simulation of life by a gentle draw as they approach the fish so that the nymph appears to be swimming up from the bottom. When he can see the fish, he watches its head, and looks for the white of the opening mouth to tell him when the nymph has been taken. This means great concentration and though he has exceptional eyesight, I think if we concentrated as much as he does on the head of the fish, and knew exactly what we were looking for, we also might see the white flicker. Nymph fishing is high concentration and knowing what to look for.

Sawyer said that, while reasonably delicate and accurate casting is obviously important, many a relatively indifferent caster is a fine fisherman and better than the man who throws a beautiful line but is not a hunter, craftily approaching and spotting his fish and knowing exactly what to try to do and what to expect. He said that it was surprising how many fishermen were careless about concealment – how they would get up cautiously into position, cast once or twice and then stand to have a better look, kneel again and cast. Or how they would get up to release their fly from some bank obstruction and then retire and kneel again, apparently oblivious of the fact that, by getting up, they had scared the fish for good.

When he saw a trout turn away from a nymph after a careful inspection, he knew it was practically useless to offer the same nymph again, though the same nymph a size smaller might be taken. He thought this was because the fish had correctly gauged the size of the nymphs then swimming. People often wondered how Sawyer manages to see so much of underwater life. 'They forget,' he said, 'that I spend much of my time in water up to my waist weed cutting or bank repairing or looking for pike, and I have every opportunity to peer down into the water and watch the life beneath.' He showed me a stone covered with hundreds of small snails, pin head size, and said that before long the trout would be feeding on them voraciously. The minnows too were spawning, collecting in hundreds on the shallows.

He pointed out a misconception about the use of fly boards – that they are useful for collecting eggs for transfer to another part of the river for re-stocking, but that they will not themselves encourage fly on a part of the river unsuited for them. He makes use of ordinary paving stones tilted up on a brick or a wooden peg with their upper edges out of water – easily moveable – the olives alight on the exposed edge and crawl down into the water to lay their eggs while the stone creates lies and shelter for trout.

He showed me where he had scooped out five and six feet holes in the river bed on a shallow stretch to provide a retreat and shelter for the trout. We could see the larger trout taking up position there; they would drop down to the shallows to feed but always had the deeper hole as a nearby sanctuary. Trout always need a feeling of security – of cover in emergency. He cuts his weeds on the same principle, leaving bars of weeds across the river at thirty-yard intervals – cover for fish, fly producing, and clear water in between for the angler. Any kind of weed is good, he said, provided it is rooted securely in the gravel.

Some years ago, said Sawyer, the river was filthy – the mud stank so that the officers' mess, three hundred yards away from the river bank, complained of the smell. The fish were dark and lank and the water had seeped into the banks and turned them into marsh. Sawyer decided that the only way to deal with this neglect – due to the war – was to put bulldozers and dragline excavators right through the river, take the filth out on to the banks, and then build up the banks and level them off. There was much anxiety and opposition on his committee to the very drastic proposal, but he persisted and started. He used to go home, he said, after watching the havoc caused by the bulldozers, desperately worried, and in a really bad way. The valley looked terrible, he said, and he sometimes wondered whether he might not be destroying the fishery for good.

For a year the banks were knee-deep mud, but now

they were beautifully level and firm and grassy. As for the machines, not only did they clear out all the stinking mud, they loosened the gravel bed of the river so that the water could come up through it and the river was aerated and the shallows made perfect spawning grounds for trout. At spawning time the shallows at Netheraven are covered with spawning fish.

It is a live, productive, natural and most beautiful river again and full of trout in perfect condition. During a heavy fall of black gnat in May, Sawyer said that in one reach alone he could see a thousand feeding fish at one time. And the hatches of fly are prodigious throughout the year. When we were there, pale wateries were coming off steadily, and fish were moving wherever we went and, in the evenings, Sawyer says, the sherry spinners fly up-stream in great clouds.

This reclamation of a fine river was impressive. I wished I had both the means and the courage to try the same experiment on portions of the Lambourn which are capable of producing as many trout of about the same average size as the Upper Avon. I went back and thoughtfully considered my stretch of the Lambourn but saw it in the most unfavourable light, with gales and high winds making fishing impossible for the rest of the month.

XVI

Sammy has Last Word

UNHAPPILY this abominable weather continued more or less to the end of the season. I see, in my last entry, for September 28th: 'Looks like last day of a season which has left the impression of bad weather, blustering downstream winds, little fly, and relatively few fish.' Well, the disappointment evident there was perhaps only natural, but after all, the little river had produced ninety-two trout in good condition, of one pound and over, and that number would have been substantially increased if we had seriously fished the may-fly. More skilful and persistent fishermen would doubtless have taken many more trout, though whether they would have enjoyed themselves any more than I did it is difficult to say.

You may argue that this particular season, chosen at random, was not really representative, but although the weather was consistently unkind, this made no real difference to the basic problems. The fishing was more difficult, and if sometimes the boisterous wind seemed unjustly severe, it simply heightened the challenge. It did, moreover, give to the kindly days, when the weather relented, a special radiance, and added to the gentle times when everything went right an aura of enchantment.

I also note that as a final record of that last day: 'Slatey grey and calm. Several big fish wallowing above hatches, but would look at nothing, though I bombarded them with every variety of nymph. At last saw one good fish follow and take. Hooked him. Had to hold him hard to keep him from hatch but he jumped suddenly and broke me. One-and-a-half pounds? Got into water to try to reach Sammy for last time. River deceptively deep, over top of thigh waders. Silt deep – too deep – could not get across.'

And so Sammy had the last word. I don't begrudge it him. He had given us such entertainment that he deserved the freedom of the river. I do, however, still detect a note of despondency in that final entry, a tinge of resignation as if I had expected the one-and-a-half pounder to break me, and the water to come trickling over the top of my waders, which is one of the most melancholy feelings in angling. I even detect in the brevity of the diary entry, and the rather careless scribble, a desire to be done with it, to retire and lick my wounds.

In retrospect, however, I know that this gloom was only momentary and superficial. There is no such thing as failure in fishing. All fishing seasons are good, though some are better than others. That is all. To be an angler you must also be an optimist. You must believe that eventually the fish will take your fly, or that the downstream wind will blow itself out, or that tomorrow conditions will be perfect.

It depends, of course, upon the kind of fishing you are engaged upon, and I think it is easier for the coarse fisherman to apply his optimism than it is for the chalk-stream angler. The coarse fisherman is generally fishing blind, so to speak, with his lure and his quarry hidden from him below the surface of the water. When the fish are not biting he can always cheer himself up by believing that the conditions will improve, or that the fish will follow his ground bait into the swim, or that they are just not feeding but will soon be ravenously hungry. The greater part of the fascination of coarse fishing lies in the mystery of what is going on down there below the surface, what monsters are approaching the cunningly presented bait, what great shoals of fish are moving in through the weed runnels to send the float sliding away into the darkness.

I have had some of my best roach fishing on the Hampshire Avon in December blizzards, when only optimism could have kept me away from a chair by the fire. If the coarse fisher knows what he is trying to do, and understands the conditions in which he is fishing, there is always a chance that he will make contact with a record-breaker. The patient anglers who set out to catch a great carp in mysterious ponds may wait for hours or for days and nights without response, but they never give up hope, and, in the end, their faith and their optimism are sometimes rewarded.

They are men with an obsession about carp; they have studied every method of presenting their bread or their potato, and they are confident that a time will come when some pig-like fish will snuffle at their bait and absorb it. They may not be certain that they will land their fish, for the carp is a tremendous fighter, but they have solved the basic problems and induced their fish to take. They are optimists because they know what they are doing, and have faith in their methods.

In chalk-stream fishing with fly or nymph, optimism has to be based on less ascertainable factors. In those clear rivers the problem, in all its complexity, is set out before you. There are days when the trout are down for good, lying dormant on the bed of the river, or concealing themselves under the weeds or the banks. I remember Lunn of Stockbridge telling me once that he reckoned that Test trout spent eighty per cent of their time in the weeds. The coarse fisher would draw the fish out of the weeds by skilful use of ground bait, but the fly fisher has to await a phenomenon of nature, a hatch of fly which will bring the trout out into the open for their meal. There is, mercifully, nothing automatic about the timing of the hatch. Nature does not function to a precise timetable and there are so many permutations and combinations causing the behaviour of fish and fly that even the most knowledgeable angler can only work on general assumptions.

We all know those days when conditions seem to be perfect, and yet the trout cussedly refuse to move. There are the other days of cruel wind and rain when it seemed that all sensible, living creatures would run for cover but when, by the same token, we took our limit in a couple of hours. These two extremes call for real optimism if they are to be coped with successfully. I have always found that the older the angler is, the more optimistic he is. The more experience, that is to say, he has at his disposal, the more resolutely he will cling to the belief that in due course a fish will rise.

XVII

A Touch of Magic

IT WOULD be interesting to calculate how much of a day with the dry fly on a chalk stream is actually spent in fishing. Surprisingly little, I would think. It is true that all our activities are conditioned by fishing – the slow progress up the river bank searching for a takeable trout, the minor entomological investigations, with or without marrow spoons and butterfly nets, the changing of flies, the avoidance of bulls or swans, the unravelling of tangles, the untying of wind knots, the freeing of flies from the small of our backs and tree branches and vegetation of one sort or another, the lighting of pipes in blustering winds, the break (and how welcome!) for sandwiches and whatever liquor we may have seen fit to put into our flasks – all these and related activities account for a considerable part of the day and to them we must add the agreeable pauses for solemn post-mortems with fellow fishers and river keepers, and the long walk back to the car.

There is not much time left for fishing itself, the putting of flies before trout. Not much time, and part of that wasted by inaccurate or clumsy casting, so that the effective presentation of the fly is seen to represent only brief interludes in a busy day on the river.

Now this may sound like the lament of a bungler. A bungler maybe, but certainly not a lamenting one. I regard all these small happenings as part of a day's fishing, from the moment when you get out of bed and draw the curtains to see which way the wind is blowing, to the time when, so many hours later, you switch out the light and proceed to dream of the one you missed under the thorn bush. The day is a sort of Bayeux Tapestry of events, all of them interwoven and taking their due place in the pattern. And the pattern is never repeated. No two days' fishing are ever precisely the same. Never a day passes without our learning something new, something about the natural life of the river, and our part in it as fisherman. It will indeed be a sad moment for us when we think we know it all.

It is true that as the years go by we worry less about our own failures and more about the misadventures of our friends. It is true also that gradually we find distraction, increasing distraction, in the background to our fishing, in the changing leaf and the snowy blossom of the ranunculus, the drumming snipe and the tumbling plover, the mewing buzzard and the white barn owl in the wood, and that the more we love and learn our background, the more richly decorated does our tapestry become. And we can recall it at will, not in every detail perhaps, but enough to set us dreaming by the fire.

When I find sleep elusive I do not count sheep. I fish in imagination up my stretch of the river, seeing with perfect clarity every yard of the way, though I am inclined, I fancy, to catch rather larger fish than usual, and I do not waste time unduly over tangled nylon or lost flies. And by the time I have landed my fourth two-pounder, I am well and truly asleep. I suppose many fishermen have discovered in their memories this same anodyne, but they may fish lordlier rivers and perhaps go wading after great salmon in the Spey or the Tweed. I should not find this so restful, and a salmon or two might well turn my dreams into nightmares. The Lambourn cannot produce nightmares. Its disasters are proportionately small, and though a lost trout may cause disappointment, it is a disappointment which never touches the profundities of a Greek tragedy. Mind you, the disappointments are sometimes momentarily severe.

I remember one lovely spring day last year when I was prospecting a fast stickle which runs below a weir pool. The stickle is nowhere more than three feet deep, but the water is well oxygenated, and usually holds several takeable fish about the pound mark. The light on the water was difficult, with the sun in my eyes, but I made out a movement in mid-stream and put a Blue Upright over it. I was taken immediately by a fish of some two pounds who jumped and threw the hook at once. This should have been a warning, but I examined the barb of my hook and all was well so that I did not hesitate to put the same fly over another small movement a little way higher up. The same thing happened again exactly – the confident rise, the feel of a heavy fish, and the line suddenly going slack, in the melancholy way it does on such occasions.

By then I was annoyed with myself and paused to think things over. What were these large fish doing in this thin water at this time of year, apart from mocking me? I would not have been so surprised at finding them there later in the summer but in April they were off their beat. While I was considering the situation, I saw a head and tail rise about three-quarters of the way across the river, and there could be no mistaking the size of that particular fish. He was in the three- to four-pound class with a shoulder on him like an ox. I hastily put the Blue Upright to him, and he had it at once, but the moment he felt the hook he was off like a fire engine, charging up the stickle, and spreading bow waves before him. Then came the awful moment. The 5x nylon, which I was unwisely using, broke just above the hook and the great trout regained the sanctuary of the weir pool. This was clearly my own fault. After the shocks of the first two fish I should have examined my cast and probably replaced it with something stouter since there were monsters about. This was a minor tragedy, and I have tried not to dream about it.

I did not, however, find it unduly depressing. Coming across those large fish in that shallow water at that time of year was so interesting that it took the sting out of my failure, and I can pass the spot now with no more than a gentle blush. It is, moreover, encouraging to have the unexpected thrown at you so weightily. It is the possibility of the improbable which keeps us on our toes.

There we have the root of it. Everything in chalk-stream fishing is improbable. Everything indeed would seem to be impossible. That a man with a small piece of split cane and a gossamer-thin cast and an implausible artificial fly should take educated trout in pellucid water, tests optimism and belief to their foundations. Our faith, however, is based upon centuries of experiment and experience, and when we tighten into a fish we are drawing upon a rich legacy bequeathed to us by fishermen down the ages. We are grateful to them for instilling in us the belief that when we stand waving what appears to be a wholly inadequate rod at wholly educated fish, we are not so foolish as it might appear.

For myself, I am convinced that there is a touch of magic about it, a magic that draws us inexorably back to the river, however unsuccessful we may be. In the world today we are quite familiar with magic, and we are inclined to shrug our shoulders at the news that a space ship has landed on the moon. Scientists have a wand to wave, and in their modest way fishermen are scientists also. They are practising biologists, however little they may recognize the fact. They are, the great ones among them, research workers of high quality and even the humbler ones who have discovered that a Greenwell is a satisfactory imitation of a dark olive in the spring, even these observers bring a clinical quality to their fishing.

When all is said and done, however, it is the simple things which strike most effectively at the fisherman's heart. The smells of the river – water, weed and marshy ground – are part of his enjoyment no less than the stalking of a fish and the casting and the hoped-for rise. Simple things – so many of them – make up the angler's true delight. And all of them may be found on the banks of the little River Lambourn.